HEIMLICH'S MANEUVERS

HEIMLICH'S MANEUVERS

My Seventy Years
of Lifesaving Innovations

HENRY J. HEIMLICH, MD

59 John Glenn Drive
Amherst, New York 14228

Published 2014 by Prometheus Books

Cover image © John Johnston, www.johnjohnston.com
Cover design by Liz Scinta
Unless otherwise noted, all images are from the author's personal collection.

Inquiries should be addressed to
Prometheus Books
59 John Glenn Drive
Amherst, New York 14228
VOICE: 716–691–0133
FAX: 716–691–0137
WWW.PROMETHEUSBOOKS.COM

18 17 16 15 14   5 4 3 2 1

Library of Congress Cataloging-in-Publication Data

Heimlich, Henry J., author.
    Heimlich's maneuvers : my seventy years of lifesaving innovation / by Henry J. Heimlich.
        p. ; cm.
    ISBN 978-1-61614-849-2 (pbk.)
    ISBN 978-1-61614-850-8 (ebook)
    I. Title.
    [DNLM: 1. Heimlich, Henry J. 2. Physicians—Autobiography. 3. Heimlich Maneuver—history. WZ 100]

RD27.35.H44
617.092--dc23
[B]

                                                                    2013036223

Printed in the United States of America

To my late wife, Jane, and my sister, Cecilia Rosenthal

CONTENTS

8   CONTENTS

FOREWORD

What can you say about a man who is innovative, talented, and caring? I would say he sounds like my doctor, Dr. Henry J. Heimlich.

In 1965, I was born with a condition called tracheoesophageal fistula, a rare birth defect that interfered with my ability to swallow and breathe normally. My condition caused serious problems. I aspirated my saliva, which could have led to pneumonia or death. I would not have been able to eat without regurgitating my food.

There was only one man who had a vision to help me: Dr. Henry J. Heimlich. I do believe God was watching over me when this man came into my life. He came up with a surgical procedure that saved my life as well as many other infants in years to come. I have the honor of having been the youngest child to have this surgery. I underwent a total of thirteen operations and was "trached" for the first five years of my life.

After that, I had a normal childhood and experienced relatively few problems. I played baseball and football in high school. At the age of eighteen, I began a career in emergency medical services, and at the age of twenty-two, I was certified as a paramedic. I have teaching credentials with the American Heart Association in advanced cardiac life support, pediatric advanced life support, and CPR (cardiopulmonary resuscitation).

At the age of forty-eight, I am still a paramedic and an emergency medical services instructor. It is because of Dr. Heimlich's dedication to helping others that I went in the medical profession. Whenever I teach the Heimlich Maneuver to my students, I tell them about the man who saved my life.

Today, I live a full life. I am happily married with five children. Ever since I was released from the hospital after undergoing Dr. Heimlich's procedure at the age of nine months, I have stayed in touch with him. I call him from time to time to let him know how I am doing, and he always responds warmly. I cannot tell you how much I love this man.

Dr. Heimlich, I will always be grateful for your gift of life.

Your patient and friend,
Guy Carpico

AUTHOR'S NOTE

There are two subjects concerning medical ethics that I would like to clarify with readers.

First, in experimenting with medical innovation, sometimes a doctor must try out an idea on patients to see if what has shown to work in a laboratory environment also works in everyday life. There have been some individuals who were the first to be treated with my procedures—procedures that had not been widely adopted yet. Every patient who has ever been involved with my research or who has undergone an experimental surgical procedure under my care had full knowledge of any risk involved and granted permission to participate.

Second, some of the experiments I conducted many years ago involved dogs. At that time, the issue of animal rights had not been fully recognized by the medical community yet. Part of the reason was that we did not have access to computer technology and modeling that today provide answers to medical questions and, therefore, eliminate the need for animal testing. I want to make clear that I strongly believe in protecting the health and safety of animals, not just in medical research but in all areas of life. If I were to conduct a medical experiment today, I would look only to solutions that do not involve animal research.

Sincerely,
Henry J. Heimlich, MD

ACKNOWLEDGMENTS

I wish to thank numerous people who have helped make this book possible.

I appreciate the staffs from the Henry J. Heimlich Archival Collection, the Henry R. Winkler Center for the History of the Health Professions, the University of Cincinnati Libraries, and the Cincinnati Public Library Information and Reference and History Departments for the expertise and proficiency exhibited researching many facets of the book.

I thank Vicki Roberts, my very capable administrative assistant, with whom I completed the first manuscript. My thanks also go to the talented writer Andrea Sattinger for her contributions.

I wish to thank Ricardo O. Ang II for his artistic skill as the photographer of my author photo and Lori Elizabeth Donnelly for her help researching and providing citations.

I wish to express my gratitude to my publicist, Melinda Zemper, who has supported me in so many ways with her intelligence and encouragement.

Dear thanks go to Karen Carmichael and Terri Lusane for helping me keep my life in order.

And thank you to my children, Elisabeth, Philip, and Janet, for their love and dedication. Elisabeth is the archivist of family photos; Philip handled legal aspects; and Janet, a published author, was so helpful with her expertise as an editor.

1

HEEEEERE'S HEIMLICH!

A number of years ago, I turned on Comedy Central and got a jolt. It was a rerun of *The Tonight Show Starring Johnny Carson*, and I was sitting on the guest couch, talking with Johnny. This was back in 1979, at the height of my fame as the inventor of the Heimlich Maneuver. I was surprised to see myself on national television, but the fact is, the maneuver I had created to save the lives of choking victims had proven so effective that it had made me a celebrity.

Figure 1.1. *Johnny and me*: It was a thrill to appear on *The Tonight Show Starring Johnny Carson* in 1979. (Photograph by Gene Arias/ NBC/NBCU Photo Bank via Getty Images.)

Before the episode starts, the Comedy Central announcer introduces it by saying, "Dr. Henry Heimlich, originator of the Heimlich Maneuver, is more than a lifesaver; he is a very funny man."

Then Johnny and I are shown seated onstage. "Would you like to demonstrate the maneuver on a doll," asks Johnny, gesturing offstage, "or on a human?"

I answer, jokingly, "I can perform it on a human . . . or on you, Johnny." His response is to hold up a finger and say, "That's one, Doctor." Much laughter from the audience.

I then describe to Johnny the symptoms of choking: the person cannot breathe or talk but can signal he is choking by placing a hand to his throat. Johnny gets in front of me, makes wild motions with his head, and points to his throat.

"Johnny," I say, "this is the first time you've been silent on the show." More laughter from the audience as Johnny holds up two fingers and says, "That's two."

Johnny then calls over the lovely Angie Dickinson and demonstrates the maneuver on her. She turns and kisses him on the lips.

I said, "I discover the maneuver and he gets the kiss!" Big laughs. Johnny holds up three fingers.

I then demonstrate how to do the maneuver on oneself by leaning over the back of a chair. I explain that I learned this from people who wrote me about having saved their own lives. "Of course they saved themselves," Johnny says, "or they couldn't have written about it."

I am confused for a moment and then hold up a finger and say, "That's one, Johnny." It brings down the house.

"Dr. Heimlich and I are appearing at the Comedy Store next week," Johnny tells his audience.

Seeing myself on national television is a very strange experience.

I ask myself, "How in the world did I, a physician, wind up on *Johnny Carson?*" How is it that I invented a lifesaving method that led to my becoming so well known? In my younger years, I never dreamed that my name would become a household word, and it was the last thing my wife wanted, a woman who had grown up with famous parents.

I think it started with a basic aspect of my personality: I have always been driven to find creative ways to solve problems; the simpler the solution, the better. I have seen medical problems and sought creative ways to fix them. If something makes sense, I say, do it. I have attacked the problem of saving lives as a creative entrepreneur, you could say, not as a company man or a guy stuck working in the laboratory day in and day out.

I enjoy the challenge of discovering creative and logical solutions to medical problems, not only in coming up with such solutions as the Heimlich Maneuver but also many others. In fact, I have invented a number of surgical procedures and medical devices that have saved, and continue to save, hundreds of thousands of lives every year.

But what makes the Heimlich Maneuver particularly special is this: while most of my other ideas were put into use by medical professionals, *the maneuver is accessible to everyone*. Because of its simplicity—and the fact that it works when performed correctly—just about anyone can save a life. People can save the life of a stranger, a neighbor, a spouse, or a child. And it can happen anywhere—in restaurants, homes, ballparks—you name it.

You see, you don't have to be a doctor to save a life. You just have to have knowledge and the instincts to respond in a crisis. I suppose I became famous because my name was associated with the maneuver, but what really got the idea going was the fact that it put in people's hands the ability to help others. It has enabled individuals to recognize that a crisis is at hand, to realize that they have the know-how to save a life, and then to act on that knowledge. And that's a very powerful thing.

I know this to be true because I myself saved a life as a "civilian," you could say, well before I became a physician. In fact, I hadn't even begun medical school. The incident happened when I was twenty-one years old and working a summer job as a camp counselor.

MY FIRST SAVE

It was late morning on August 28, 1941, and I was riding a train from Lee, Massachusetts, to New York City. I had been teaching sailing to children at Camp Mah-Kee-Nac, and now 254 campers, staff members, and I were on our way home after a great summer vacation.

Figure 1.2. *Camp counselor at age twenty-one:* In 1941, I taught children sailing at Camp Mah-Kee-Nac in Massachusetts.

All was well as we sped up to Hatch Pond in northwestern Connecticut. Many of the kids were enjoying their lunches. They were singing and laughing, excited to be on their way home. Suddenly, the train ground to a halt and everyone went flying forward. A quick assessment told me that the campers were shaken up, but no one appeared to be injured. We were in the rear of the train. I ran into the next forward car and knew something had gone severely wrong. This car was tilted, and strangely so. But again, everyone seemed okay.

I jumped out of the train and could not believe what I saw. The four cars ahead were completely off the tracks. The locomotive's engine had been ripped off and was sitting in the pond. (Later, I learned that two engineers had died, trapped in the cab of the submerged engine.) One of the last two cars, where the children and I had been sitting, remained largely undisturbed.

I ran forward, making my way around the disjointed cars. Then something caught my eye. At the base of the second car, I saw a man struggling frantically in four or five feet of water, his head submerged. I jumped in the cold, murky water and swam over to him. I lifted his shoulders to raise up his head. The man coughed and spat out water. His face was blackened with coal dust, and he was crying.

I tried to move him, but it was no use—his right leg was caught in the dirt under the steps of the train car. I could think of nothing more to do than hold the man's head above the water and hope that help would arrive soon.

The man was in tremendous pain, so I tried to engage him in conversation to take his mind off it. He told me his name was Otto Klug, and he was a fireman on the train, the crewperson who shovels the coal that runs the engine. He had leapt from the engine to avoid injury before becoming pinned under the water. To give him some kind of relief, I used the pond water to clean his soot-covered face.

When Mr. Klug found out I was about to be a medical student, he started asking me questions about his condition.

"Am I okay?" he asked fearfully. "Am I going to live?"

"I'm sure you'll be fine," I said.

"Am I going to lose my leg?"

I didn't know what to say. I was quite sure that the answer was yes, but I did not want Mr. Klug to give up hope.

The police and medical personnel finally arrived. By that time, Mr. Klug and I had been in the water for two hours, and we were both shivering. When doctors suggested that they immediately amputate Mr. Klug's leg, he begged them not to. I suggested that they give him morphine, which they did. After that, he calmed down.

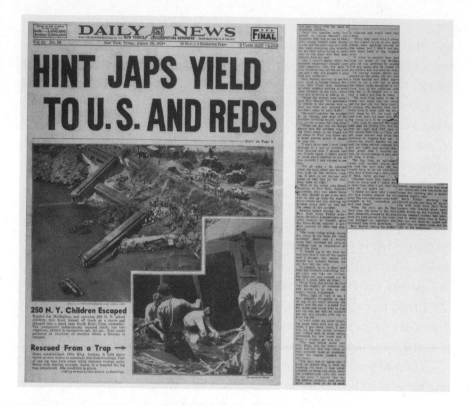

Figure 1.3. *My first save*: A crew of people and I desperately try to free Otto Klug, whose leg is pinned under the train car. I believe that is me, with my back to the camera, holding a shovel. (From "Rescued from a Trap," *New York Daily News*, Friday, August 29, 1941.)

Meanwhile, the car was slipping deeper and deeper into the mud. The crew had to act fast. They tied a sheet to the train and ran it under Mr. Klug's back to hold him above the water. Welders used acetylene torches underwater to cut away the steel so that the man could be freed. Seeing that Mr. Klug was in good hands, I returned to the campers, and the press swarmed around us. Mr. Klug was taken to a hospital where his leg was amputated below the knee.

The next day, my father and mother, Philip and Mary Heimlich, were in a hotel in Chicago on the way to visit relatives in Denver. Of course, they had no idea what had happened. The morning after the train wreck, they bought

HEEEEERE'S HEIMLICH!   23

a copy of the *New York Times*. Mom saw the front-page story of the train crash and read my name and fainted. When she came to, Dad read her the story, and she learned her only son was alive and well.

A month later, I appeared again in the *Times*, this time in an article whose caption read, "Henry Heimlich of Cornell University Medical College accepting from Frank L. Jones, president of the Greater New York Safety Council, the annual prize, a gold watch, for his calmness and courage in saving a life in a railroad wreck near South Kent, Conn."[1] The article shows a photo of me, beaming, as I accept the award.

Figures 1.4 and 1.5. *Recognized*: I accept a watch as an award for saving the life of Otto Klug. (Figure 1.5 *[right]* from "Children Escape in Train Wreck; 2 of Crew Killed," *New York Times*, Friday, August 29, 1941.)

Now that I think about it, that recognition was my first brush with fame. Accounts of the accident called me a "hero." But, even back then, I could not have cared less about the attention. Otto Klug was alive, and that's all that mattered.

What I could not have known at the time was that there would be many more Otto Klugs—individuals whose lives I would save using a combination of medical expertise and common sense. And with those experiences would come immense satisfaction from knowing that I was able to help sustain life. But there would be many challenges, too, for I was to learn that the field of medicine was not only a fascinating discipline from which amazing ideas sprout, but that it is also a political minefield.

2

MY BEGINNINGS

Saving lives begins with wanting to help people, just as I had wanted to help Otto Klug on that summer day in 1941. I attribute my desire to help others to my parents.

Philip and Mary Heimlich taught me that the highest calling in life is to serve others, even when life poses very difficult challenges. My father was a social worker and a pioneer in the rehabilitation of delinquent youth and convicts in prison—individuals on whom society had given up. He founded the Youth Counsel Bureau, which began as an interfaith project to assist youths who were in trouble with the law, and he worked for the Jewish Board of Guardians for thirty years. My mother grew up in a poor family and lost her mother when she was a teenager, yet she understood the value of hard work, sacrifice, and taking responsibility. Both of my parents believed in the importance of family.

Mom and Dad were the most generous people I have ever known. They devoted their lives to helping others, sometimes in big ways and sometimes by simply offering a listening ear. When we lived in New Rochelle, New York, where I grew up, there were always relatives staying with us. At one point, my mother's five brothers and sisters lived with us. When the Great Depression hit, family members who had lost everything they owned knew they had a place to stay at Phil and Mary's. My parents even took in my consumptive aunt until they found a facility that could properly care for her. All types of people with all kinds of problems came to see my parents. One night, it might have been a senator or a judge; the next night, an ex-con. At the end of his life, Dad lived with us. Even as he neared his one hundredth birthday, people still called and came to see him to discuss their problems and seek his advice.

Figure 2.1. *My parents*: Philip and Mary Heimlich were the most generous people I have ever known.

Figure 2.2. *A lively home*: People from all walks of life came to visit us and to seek advice from my parents.

"Pop" (as we called him) was born on April 26, 1887. From the time he was a child, he had a very bad stutter. He despaired of getting a job after graduating from the then tuition-free City College of New York, now City University, in 1909. Around that time, he met a girl named Mary Epstein, whom he liked very much.

Mary was born on May 23, 1892, and was the eldest of six children. She had had a difficult time growing up. Her mother died in 1906, when Mary was only a teenager, and so she was left to take care of her five younger siblings, which included an infant. Her father remarried, hoping to provide a mother for his six children. The entire family—including relatives of Mary's stepmother—moved into a small apartment in a poor Jewish neighborhood on the Lower East Side of New York City. Altogether, there were ten people living in the apartment.

Figure 2.3. *My mother*: Mary Epstein cared for her five younger siblings after their mother died.

Mary had hoped that having a stepmother would make her life and the lives of her siblings easier. Instead, the opposite was true. The stepmother was abusive and frequently beat my mother and her brothers and sisters. When her father realized what was going on, he moved all six children into a separate apartment. He supported them, although he stayed with his wife's family. My mother, at the age of sixteen, was determined to raise her five brothers and sisters and to keep them together.

Pop knew nothing of this, only that he enjoyed spending time with Mary. However, because she was always surrounded by five children, he assumed she was married and was hesitant to ask her out. Another reason for his hesitation was that Pop was still nervous about his stutter. His college advisor was sympathetic. One day, she pulled him aside and suggested he get a job out of town, in a place where no one knew him, "and don't tell them you stutter," she advised. "Each time before you speak, take a deep breath, make up your mind not to stutter, and explode!"

With best wishes
Phil Heimlich
Taken Sept. 27, 1911

Figure 2.4. *My father:* Philip Heimlich struggled with a stuttering problem but learned how to overcome it.

After graduating from college, Pop was offered an instructor's position in architectural drafting at Rose Polytechnic Institute (now the Rose-Hulman Institute of Technology) in Terre Haute, Indiana. The Midwest seemed like another country for a Jewish kid from the Bronx, but he remembered the words of his college advisor and decided to give it a try. Before he left for Indiana, Pop was told some other enlightening information. A friend let him know that Mary Epstein was not married, that the children she cared for were her siblings.

After a short courtship, Pop proposed to Mary and asked her to move west with him. She turned down his proposal because she felt obligated to continue to care for her siblings, so Pop went on to Indiana. While at Rose Polytech, he was determined to end his nagging stutter. Pop practiced his college advisor's take-a-breath-and-explode method, and it worked. He was thrilled about this personal victory, but he also was homesick. Pop missed his hometown and his girl, so, after teaching at the institute for one year, he returned to New York City.

When Pop returned to New York, he again proposed to Mary, and this time she said yes. Mary was still taking care of her siblings when she accepted my father's proposal, but the couple hit upon a good arrangement: Pop had decided to give up architecture and instead become a social worker. He and Mary would be cottage parents at the Hawthorne Reform School, part of the Jewish Board of Guardians in Hawthorne, New York. In those days, young boys who got into trouble were sent to the reform school until they were old enough to work. Mary boarded out her younger siblings to people living in the vicinity of the school, and her two older brothers were employed and remained in New York City. In the end, Mary's brothers and sisters all grew up to lead successful and productive lives, a testament to the way she raised and nurtured them. A few years later, Pop took a job in Wilmington, Delaware, to be director of the Young Men's Hebrew Association, the Jewish counterpart of the Young Men's Christian Association (YMCA). On May 31, 1914, my sister was born. Philip and Mary named her Cecilia, but we all called her "Cele."

I was my parents' second child, born on February 3, 1920, and was given the name Henry Judah Heimlich.

Figure 2.5. *My sister*: Cecilia Heimlich was born in 1914. (Photograph courtesy of Cecilia Rosenthal.)

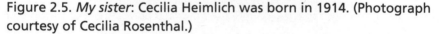

We were still living in Wilmington at the time, but a year after my birth, my father got a job with the Jewish Board of Guardians in New York City. Rather than move back to the city, we settled in New Rochelle. We could barely afford the suburbs, but my parents felt that Cele and I would get a better education there. The move proved to be more than just a financial sacrifice for Pop: To start his day, he had to walk several miles to get to the train station in downtown New Rochelle, where he boarded the train for New York City. After work, he would again walk several miles from the train station to our home.

We lived in a four-bedroom house in New Rochelle. A stream ran in front of our house. When I was three or four years old, Mom would place me beside the stream and let me hold a string with a clothespin tied at the end, dangling in the water. Years later, she laughed and told me I thought I was fishing. Cele, who is six years my senior, has told me that I would sit there for hours, daydreaming. Even as an adult, I have been told I daydream. But it's a good thing. In fact, on more than one occasion, I have come up with a ground-breaking medical discovery after a nice bout of daydreaming.

Figure 2.6. *A baby*: I was born on February 3, 1920.

Figure 2.7. *A happy childhood*: I grew up in New Rochelle, New York, where I enjoyed daydreaming by the stream that ran in front of our house.

AN EARLY INNOVATION

Growing up in New Rochelle, I grew to love the water. I used to go swimming at the Hudson Park public beach on the Long Island Sound. I adored watching the boats and wished that one day I could have one for my very own. My love of the water led to an early attempt at innovation and a lesson in rejection by my peers.

When I was about ten years old, I saw a child floating on a makeshift raft made from three boards that came together to form a triangle. Under each of the three corners of the triangle, an inflated ball was attached, allowing the raft to float. The boy sat on one of the corners and paddled his way down the sound. It looked like a lot of fun.

On my way home from the beach, I could not stop thinking about the boy paddling along and got an idea to build my own boat, similar to the one he had. I went to our basement and found three boards, each about five feet long, and nailed the ends of the boards together to form a triangle. I then found three empty, rectangular motor-oil cans, making sure to screw tight the cap of each container to ensure that no water could get in. Each can had a hinged handle, which I used to nail a can to each corner of my vessel.

In no time, I had completed my replica of the boy's raft. I stepped inside the triangle and lifted the raft so that it encircled me, and I grabbed a small board that would serve as a paddle. Paddle in hand and sort of wearing my raft, I walked three blocks to a nearby inlet. I attracted the attention of most of the neighborhood kids who followed me; we were all excited to see if my invention would work. When we got to the inlet, I walked into the slimy water.

The raft wasn't very sturdy, but it floated. But rather than cheer on my success, a few of the kids who had followed me thought it would be fun to throw stones at my boat. They aimed rocks at the cans that held me afloat until they started pulling away from the boards. The raft came apart, and my maiden voyage came to an end. As I journeyed back to my house, carrying what was left of my vessel, I felt both proud and discouraged. I had accomplished what I had set out to do but was sad to see my invention destroyed.

I had no idea then that the stone-throwing incident would later serve as a metaphor for what I endured when I became a medical inventor. Sadly, people with new ideas are often attacked, sometimes for no reason other than the critics do not like someone else getting credit. Just as the boys tried to destroy my invention by throwing stones, some of my future naysayers would also try to sink my ideas.

I knew I wanted to be a doctor since before I started grammar school. I remember our family physician, Dr. Belle Jacobson, coming to make house calls. In those days, it was extremely unusual for women to become physicians. Dr. Jacobson was a very small woman, but when she entered the vestibule, she completely took over and filled us with a sense of confidence. I admired the way her calm and in-charge demeanor put us all at ease and made us feel that the family member she was treating would be all right. I fantasized that one day I would be like Dr. Jacobson and that I would discover a surgical operation no one else could perform.

When I was in high school, my role model was Dr. Edward Jenner, a British physician born in 1749 and who is considered today to be the father of immunology.[1] Jenner, who lived in the English countryside with his family, had heard a farmer's tale that milkmaids sometimes contracted cowpox from milking cows. (Cowpox is a disease that causes patients to develop lesions. It is similar to smallpox but much less virulent.) What's more, Jenner understood that milkmaids who got cowpox seemed never to develop smallpox. This was an important observation at that time, as smallpox was wiping out much of the world's population.

In 1796, Jenner was eager to test the efficacy of cowpox as a vaccine, and he inoculated an eight-year-old boy named James Phipps with cowpox matter taken from the pus-filled lesions on the finger of a milkmaid. Phipps developed a few cowpox lesions that were not serious. About a month later, Jenner injected young Phipps with the smallpox virus. Of course, such an experiment would be considered unacceptable according to today's standards of medical ethics. Still, Jenner's vaccine worked—the boy did not get smallpox.

A year after inoculating James Phipps, Jenner reported the results of his experiment to the Royal Society, but the paper was rejected. Undeterred, Jenner tested more cases and then privately published a small book on his procedure, which he then called *vaccination* (which comes from the Latin *vacca*, meaning "cow").

But Jenner continued to struggle to find support from his British peers. When he went to London to locate more volunteers to be vaccinated, he could not find any, so he looked to other European countries for volunteers. As more and more people were vaccinated, smallpox cases dramatically declined. In 1802, and then again in 1807, the British Parliament awarded Jenner a total of £30,000 for his innovation. Still, Britons paid a price for British doctors objecting to vaccination, for those who were denied inoculations were left susceptible to the deadly smallpox.

As a boy, I dreamed that someday I could come up with ideas that were as innovative as Jenner's. I was naïve to assume that if I could accomplish such a thing, then my colleagues would treat me better than his had treated him.

3

THE DEPRESSION, ANTI-SEMITISM, AND VISITS TO SING SING PRISON

I learned more from my father than I ever learned in school. I grew up in New Rochelle, New York, during the Great Depression, and money was tight, so I learned the importance of a dollar. But my father also taught me that money wasn't everything. As a social worker with the Jewish Board of Guardians, Pop dedicated his life to helping convicts and delinquents, a calling that brought him respect and deep satisfaction. He visited and advised Jewish convicts who were incarcerated in New York State prisons, as well as some held in a mental hospital; Pop visited each inmate several times a year. When the convicts were about to be discharged, he helped them adapt to life on the outside and frequently got them jobs in companies owned by his friends. The job paid only $2,000 a year. To better support our family, Pop took a second job at night working in the post office, then later he ran a printing company, all while he continued to help convicts. Despite the long hours, he never complained.

As with most families, the Depression hit my family unexpectedly. It happened when I was beginning high school. At the time, I did not fully understand how the country's devastated economy affected my family, but things became clearer when my mother sent me on a strange errand one day. She gave me a note and key and told me to deliver it to the vice president at the People's Bank for Savings in downtown New Rochelle. As I handed the banker the note and the key, he kindly said to me, "Tell your mother I am sorry this had to happen." Shortly thereafter, we moved out of our house, for I had delivered to the banker the key to our home and a note explaining that we couldn't pay the mortgage. We soon rented another house, larger and more attractive than the house we had owned, and remained there until I finished high school.

Despite our financial problems, my parents did their best to have enough food on hand so we could share it with others. Every Sunday, the entire family, including my aunts, uncles, and cousins who lived in New Rochelle, would come to our house for dinner. Sometimes my mother prepared roast beef and brown potatoes, or the men drove to the center of town to the kosher delicatessen to buy pastrami and corned beef for a deli supper. Since my parents spent so much attention on other family members and even strangers who came through our house, I sometimes felt neglected. When people spoke so glowingly of my parents, it made me a bit jealous, although I later appreciated just how wonderful it was to grow up in a house that was filled with love and care.

ANTI-SEMITISM

Our middle-class neighborhood in New Rochelle was unusual for the times in that there were people of mixed nationalities and religions. For example, the father of my friend Steve Kovaks was a Swedish immigrant who owned a beauty salon and barbershop. The Emanuels, who were from Greece, owned a shoe-repair business. And there were three or four Jewish families in our neighborhood. My grammar school was a melting pot, too.

Still, our community experienced the same type of prejudice that was common in the 1930s. Specifically, prejudice against Jews. In school, Jewish children were sidelined. The principal read Christian prayers during assembly. And in December, many school activities were given a Christmas theme. (We Jews quietly resisted, however. When the class sang Christmas carols, we substituted the name "Moses" for Christ and "Chanukah" for Christmas.)

When I was in my young teens, my mother asked if I would prefer to use a middle name other than Judah. I believe she was attempting to protect me from the harm that might have come from having a Jewish-sounding name. In those days, Jews were denied work and acceptance into college simply because of their faith. I followed my mother's advice when I was in high school and changed my middle name to "Jay." (About twenty years ago, I went back to my original name. Today I proudly call myself Henry Judah Heimlich.)

In high school, there were fraternities for Jews and non-Jews. I joined Omega Delta because it was known as a "nonsectarian" fraternity, which meant it accepted members of any religion. I believed in this open policy but was disappointed to find that, in reality, the fraternity was mostly Jewish with only one Christian member. While I was aware that Jews were discriminated against, African Americans were totally isolated and given few social or business opportunities. Seeing this unfairness soon after I joined Omega Delta, I decided I would avoid any segregated organizations and stopped attending fraternity meetings.

My sister Cele experienced a more direct kind of anti-Semitism than I. As the top student in her elementary school, she was entitled to receive a certificate of honor at her graduation. So we were shocked to learn that another student would be receiving the certificate. When my parents asked the principal why my sister was not the designated winner, she told them that she had instituted a new rule. That is, students would be measured not just on grades but also on attendance, and, the principal noted, Cele had been absent two days for the Jewish holidays.

My parents were convinced that the principal had jimmied the system so that the award would not be given to a Jewish child, yet they held their tongues. In those days, Jews tended to keep quiet when confronted with prejudice. Fortunately, things did not turn out as the principal had allegedly planned. Cele's name had been printed on the program before the principal changed the rules, so she was indeed handed the reward at her graduation.

Given the way kids were separated by religion in those days, I primarily socialized with Jewish people. But I broke out of that pattern when I was a junior in high school and joined the New Rochelle High School drama club, the Tower Players. Mind you, I was never a great actor, but I enjoyed performing in plays. Acting helped me develop a comfort with addressing an audience, and it brought out my sense of humor. I was given some pretty good parts. My favorite was having a role in the dramatic play *Yellow Jack*, the story of Walter Reed, the US Army doctor who saved thousands of lives after discovering that yellow fever was spread by mosquitoes.

Being part of a group comprised of both Jews and non-Jews was rewarding. One Saturday evening, after the play's last performance, the entire cast went out together to celebrate. Several of us piled into a Model T Ford convertible, bound for the Glen Island Casino in New Rochelle. We all had a great time. For this one evening, religious beliefs and social limitations were cast aside.

Still, it was rare when I spent time with non-Jews and was not made to feel self-conscious about my religion. Ultimately, my experiences with anti-Semitism and observing racial segregation made me angry. But I would turn that anger into hard work and learn to rely on my own record rather than the opinions of those who judged people by their religion or skin color.

PRISON TIME

Spending time with my father expanded my education far beyond the classroom. From the time I was twelve years old, I occasionally accompanied Dad on his travels to visit inmates and prison administrators. As I got older, my father gave me the opportunity to interact with these hardcore convicts and juvenile delinquents. It proved to be a great lesson in how to deal with people in desperate need.

As a social worker with the Jewish Board of Guardians, Dad visited Jewish prisoners in all the New York State prisons, counseling them on how to maintain hope and dignity while incarcerated and assisting them as they adjusted to the outside world when released. One of his goals was to help them stay in touch with their families for support and encouragement. If a prisoner was from New York City, Dad would try to have him sent to Sing Sing Correctional Facility in Ossining, New York, which was located on the east bank of the Hudson River. This allowed the inmates to receive more visits from family members who would not have to make a long trip to see them. I can remember making trips not only to Sing Sing but also to the Attica and Auburn prisons. I visited Mattewan State Hospital for the "criminally insane," where I peered through the small windows in the doors of padded, solitary-confinement cells to see inmates wearing straitjackets.

Figure 3.1. *A social worker*: My father worked in prisons, helping inmates who were about to be released adjust to life on the outside.

On one visit to Sing Sing, all the prisoners were assembled in the auditorium, and Dad spoke to them, describing sights and scenes in New York City. The purpose was to give them hope by providing them with positive visions of what life could be like after they had served their time. I was sitting in the middle of the audience, along with the prisoners, listening to Pop's words. He described the vaudeville show being performed at the Radio City Music Hall that cost twenty-five cents and included the dancing line of girls known as the Rockettes, comedians, magicians, and a movie. I heard an inmate next to me say, "Wow! I get out in two years. That's the first place I'm going."

Most of the prisoners respected my father so much that they looked out for him. He told me once that a prisoner had asked him to do something illegal but that Dad refused. The man then threatened to kill Dad. When other prisoners overheard the remark, they threatened to kill the prisoner, but Dad told them to forget it.

Occasionally, Cele went with us to the prisons. When I was twelve years old, she was eighteen and very pretty. Yet, despite the potential danger, Cele and I were allowed to wander unaccompanied through the prison. Sometimes a guard escorted us through the halls. He would insert his big key, unlocking the heavy steel doors that led from one hall to another. As we passed through, the doors slammed loudly behind us. From time to time, a guard left an inmate's cell door open so we could go inside and have a chat with him. I once sat in the electric chair, the method of execution used at the time in New York State, and tried to comprehend its grave purpose.

One day, after our customary walk through Sing Sing, Cele and I returned to the warden's office. Warden Lewis E. Lawes became very well known as the author of the book *Twenty Thousand Years in Sing Sing*, which in 1932 was made into a movie starring Spencer Tracy and Bette Davis. Talking with the warden that day was a state prison commissioner who noticed us kids and asked Lawes, "How can you allow these children to walk through this prison alone?" Lawes stated matter-of-factly, "All the men know these are Phil Heimlich's kids." That was all that had to be said.

What I learned from Dad on these visits—and from the way he and my mother reached out to people—was the power of respect. In the prisons, Pop had respect for the prisoners and their problems; they, in turn, had respect for him and the advice he gave. While most of society had ignored these people and their problems, my father did the opposite and taught me to do the same. In going to the prisons with Dad, I saw firsthand how respecting others—even individuals who had hit upon hard times—leads to a better life, not just for the recipients of that respect, but for us all.

In later years, I would medically treat individuals who were wealthy and powerful as well as those who came from abject poverty, both in this country and in remote areas of the world. To me, no one deserved more or less care than the other. To me, each patient was a human being, someone who needed my focused attention along with a pat on the hand and a warm smile. Many patients have let me know that they appreciated how I treated them, not just medically, but personally.

It was my parents who taught me what it means to be a compassionate physician. My experiences in the prisons were real-life lessons in dealing with individuals in need. But Dad knew exactly what he was doing. He put me in those situations out of love for me and to open my eyes to the world beyond the suburbs. He never for one minute thought that I was in danger because he himself worked in those environments every day.

One time, a friend asked Dad, "Phil, weren't you afraid of leaving Henry in such a place?"

Dad answered with a smile, "He turned out okay, didn't he?"

I guess I did.

4

MEDICAL-SCHOOL CHALLENGES AND A STRANGE INTERNSHIP

I graduated from high school in 1937 at the age of seventeen. Thankfully, I had won a New York State Regents scholarship, which gave me the chance to go to my first-choice college, Cornell University in Ithaca, New York.

Figure 4.1. *High school*: I knew from a very early age that I wanted to be a doctor.

It was a busy time. To make extra money, I worked for the National Youth Administration, typing excerpts from reference books for a zoology professor. I lived in an inexpensive rooming house instead of joining a fraternity. Back then, fraternities were segregated—not only by race but also by religion—and I did not want to isolate myself by joining a Jewish fraternity.

Cornell required all male students to receive military training through the Reserve Officers Training Corps (ROTC) or join the ROTC Cornell "freshman" marching band. The latter appealed to me more; I adored music. I had played clarinet in the New Rochelle High School band and enjoyed marching at football games. In the summer between high school and college, Dad surprised me with a baton, and so I learned how to twirl it and conduct. I tried out for the position of drum major and was selected. I was excited to be leading my college marching band my freshman year. In my second year, I was assistant drum major of the one-hundred-member, nonmilitary Cornell marching band for upperclassmen. I had high hopes that I would be the head drum major during my third year at Cornell. I loved being a drum major and wanted to be able to list this senior position on my application for medical school. Instead, though, the faculty bandmaster selected another fellow to be head drum major over me, and so I was given a secondary position in which I marched behind him, wearing a less impressive uniform. The drum major was atrocious at the job: he didn't get his signals right and so the band marched out of formation. At the first football game of the season, his direction was so poor, band members were bumping into each other. After that, the bandmaster appointed me as head drum major, and I remained in that position for the rest of the year.

It was 1939, which marked the best year Cornell's football team ever had. At the end of the season, we were undefeated and had four all-American players. We went to Columbus, Ohio, where we beat the national powerhouse college, Ohio State. At halftime, I led the band through some complicated maneuvers and we got a roaring cheer. That evening, the ROTC sergeant who oversaw the band program took me and two other band members to an after-hours bar for drinks. Once he loosened up, the sergeant told me that the bandmaster had initially chosen the other student to be head drum major over me because I was Jewish. Then, after all the foul-ups the student caused, the sergeant said the bandmaster had no choice but to make me head drum major.

Figures 4.2 and 4.3. *Leading the band*: I was the drum major for Cornell University.

CHALLENGES OF ENTERING MEDICAL SCHOOL

Even before I got into college, I knew I wanted to go to medical school and then become a doctor. Part of this was not by choice since, back in the 1930s, anti-Semitism drew lines between what Jewish people could and could not do for a living. For example, Jews were largely barred from working in upper-management positions of corporations or the government. If they had start-up money, Jews could open their own businesses. They were also accepted as lawyers or doctors. Becoming a doctor, in particular, held prestige. There's an old joke about a young Jewish mother wheeling her baby boy in a carriage: when another woman looks into the carriage and remarks about how cute the baby is, the mother beams, "That's my son, the doctor."

Figure 4.4. *A graduate*: After graduating from Cornell University, I was eager to attend Cornell Medical College.

I decided I would apply to three outstanding medical schools—Cornell Medical College (now Weill Cornell Medical College), Yale University, and New York University. And I applied in my junior year, hoping to start medical school a year early. I was eager to learn everything I could about medicine, and I knew that medical schools accepted some outstanding students after they had completed their junior year.

But getting into medical school was extremely competitive in the 1930s, especially for Jewish students. Colleges had unstated quotas as to the number of Jews they would admit. Administrators kept these numbers small to appease anti-Semitic alumni and students. Tragically, such discrimination created a fight-for-the-crumbs kind of situation for Jewish candidates. There was no question that if I wanted to be accepted into a good medical school, I would have to stand out in some way, and so I made it my goal to get a recommendation from a notable professor.

As a freshman in college, I was assigned an advisor who would counsel me throughout the duration of my undergraduate studies. Hans Bethe was a physics professor, renowned in his field. In fact, in 1967, he won the Nobel Prize in physics.[1] But, knowing where I was headed, I felt it would be better to have an advisor who was a medical doctor. I flipped through the faculty directory and noticed that there were only a few physicians on the faculty. I found a prominent anthropology professor who was a doctor of medicine and asked him if he would be my advisor. He accepted the request on the condition that my present advisor agreed, which he did. Later, I took his anthropology course and found it to be one of my favorite classes. Learning so much about the origins of humankind, as well as its physical and cultural development, biology, social customs, and beliefs was fascinating. The anthropology professor wrote me a strong recommendation for medical school.

In 1941, when I was a junior, I learned that I had achieved my goal: I had received early acceptance to all three of the medical schools to which I had applied. There was no question that I would go to Cornell in New York City. Attending a local school would allow me to live at home with my parents on Ninetieth Street. I could save money living at home, and I would get to spend more time with Mom and Dad. There were other benefits, too. Staying in the Cornell school system meant that I could apply the last year of my four-year undergraduate scholarship to my first year at Cornell Medical College.

Only after I entered my freshman year of medical school did I fully appreciate just what a feat it had been to be admitted. As I had suspected, I was one of very few Jewish students whom the school had let in. Because of the social workings on campus, we Jewish freshman easily sought each other out. There were four of us out of a class of eighty-five students.

A MEDICAL-SCHOOL STUDENT

I loved medical school. It was exciting to study the miracles of the human body. Back then, anatomy was a one-year course—versus the six weeks that it is today—and so there was a great deal to learn and digest. The studies were a lot of work, but I enjoyed every minute of it. To me, the body was a fascinating, logical system, and I was thrilled at the prospect of someday being able to improve that system when something went wrong.

I wasn't always serious about the work, though. To combat the intensity of studying, I relied on my sense of humor to keep up my spirits and everyone else's.

There was one joke I learned in medical school and used later when I gave talks. I would tell a made-up story about a patient who was severely ill and dying and under my care. His two devoted sons stayed at his bedside constantly. One day, all of the patient's symptoms improved, as did his laboratory findings. I realized he would recover and told his two sons. They asked, "When do you think he might come home?" When I told them he would be on an oxygen mask for a few days and could return home about a week later, they were overjoyed. When I left, they ran over to their father's bed and told him the good news. Suddenly, the patient sat up, gasping, and turned blue. He picked up a pad and pencil and wrote a few words. One son said, "See what he wrote!" The other son read aloud, "You're standing on my oxygen tube."

There was another funny about a man who was told by his doctor that he had contracted a terrible disease and had only one day to live. The distraught man came home, looked at his wife, and said, "Darling, this is our last night together because tomorrow I'll be dead. Let's paint the town! We'll go to our favorite restaurant for dinner, then catch a show from front-row seats, followed by a nightcap at that speakeasy we like. What do you think?"

The woman looked at him, perturbed, and said, "That's easy for you to say. You don't have to get up in the morning!"

But while I enjoyed medical school, I faced additional challenges. This period represented the worst years of anti-Semitism in US history. In fact, the largest indoor Nazi rally in the world was held at Madison Square Garden in New York City shortly before the United States entered World War II.

Mind you, most people are blind to racism and anti-Semitism unless they are the scapegoats. Such prejudice is often quite subtle. I remember one incident that occurred when three other medical students and I were taking turns dissecting a cadaver. I was taking the lead on the assignment when one fellow pointed out that I was Jewish and, therefore, did not deserve to be in charge. As strange as it sounds, he actually thought that by saying this anti-Semitic comment, he was helping me. "You should stay in the background and be quiet," he continued.

It is not in my nature to back down under pressure or compromise my position to attain a less-than-just decision. And so I held my ground. "You think Jews should stand back and take abuse. I'm as good as you are," I told him. I remember thinking that, in rebuking the student, I took after my father, who stood up for prisoners whom he felt had been treated unfairly.

JOINING THE NAVY

After the attack on Pearl Harbor on December 7, 1941, the government required that medical-school students join the military to ensure that there would be medical personnel in the field. Because I had always loved the water, I chose to join the US Navy Reserve as an unpaid ensign.

I was proud to have given an oath to fight in the war if needed, but others did not know that, because I did not wear a uniform in public. During this time, I traveled across town every day by bus, going from our home to medical school and back again. As the war progressed, there were plenty of insults hurled at me on that bus by people who did not know that I'd signed up to fight in the war if needed. Bus drivers who were too old to be drafted were particularly vicious with their comments. A typical mumbled remark was "Get on, 4F." The military designation "4F" was given to young men with physical disabilities that prevented them from being drafted into the service.

I was so incensed by people's false allegations of reserve soldiers that I wrote to Eleanor Roosevelt, who wrote a daily newspaper column. I told her how difficult it was to be in that situation. I like to think that she picked up on my comment, because, in a future column, she wrote about how people should not make assumptions regarding men who were out of uniform.

On May 7, 1943, during my last semester in medical school, the federal government created the V-12 Navy College Training Program to keep in school those students who were preparing to become officers. I was required by the federal government to resign as an ensign and become a V-12 midshipman. This time, I wore the uniform and got paid. What's more, the navy paid for my tuition. Things were looking up. Not only did I not have to put up with people's insults, but I was also admitted into officers clubs, where I could get dates with society girls.

Figure 4.5. An officer: As a midshipman, I proudly wore my uniform in public.

Figure 4.6. *Joining the navy*: There was no question that I would join the navy while in medical school because I loved the water.

A MEDICAL INTERN

In December of 1943, I graduated from medical school six months early because there were no vacations or breaks from school during the war. We just studied straight through. After that, I received an internship at Boston City Hospital and was placed on inactive duty. I was thrilled about working as a doctor in the real world, although it was a financial strain. Unlike today, when interns receive a modest salary, I was expected to work for free.

Figure 4.7. *Ready to treat patients*: After graduating from Cornell Medical College, I was excited to work as an intern in a hospital.

Working as an intern at a city hospital during the war was an odd experience—one that likely put some patients at risk. Normally, there would be plenty of physicians to offer instruction, but with so many doctors overseas, we interns were often on our own at the hospitals. (Meanwhile, those who stayed behind, which included mostly older physicians, made a lot of money. With hardly any competition, their practices flourished and they each made a fortune. I recall visiting one surgeon in Boston and seeing patients lined up down the steps and into the hall.)

Many of us interns were fresh out of medical school. We were eager to put what we had learned to use, but we needed more supervision than was given to us. We were often performing procedures that would have been better left in the hands of more experienced medical personnel. One of the first surgical operations I performed was an appendectomy, a procedure I had never done before. What's more, I had to be prepared to do it singlehandedly.

I began prepping the patient by shaving his abdomen. Next, I placed him on a rickety stretcher and wheeled him through the rat-infested tunnels under the enormous hospital that led to the operating-room building, a distance of about three blocks. Once I got to the operating room, I turned the patient on his side and injected spinal anesthesia. I knew I needed assistance, so I phoned my fellow intern on call to come and help me. While I waited for him to arrive, I painted the patient's abdomen with a pink sterilizing solution, draped sterile sheets around the site of the incision, and made my first cut. When the intern arrived, he and I set to continuing the procedure. Thankfully, we two neophytes got the appendix out. Afterward, I wheeled the patient back through the dungeons and to the ward. It was not an ideal situation for either surgeon or patient, but such experiences and responsibilities were preparing me for what I would endure in just a short time, when I would be working as a surgeon in one of the most remote places on earth.

On September 13, 1944, I was ordered back to active duty as a lieutenant JG, or junior grade, and transferred to the Chelsea Naval Hospital in Chelsea, Massachusetts. The assignment was luxurious. As an officer, I was fed delicious steak dinners, a delicacy denied most civilians during wartime. But again, the work was no picnic. With so many young men away, I, as a surgeon, had to do just about everything myself. And, as in Boston City Hospital, I was left to take on responsibilities I was not fully qualified for.

One day, I was assigned to give anesthesia to a patient undergoing a knee operation. Like performing the appendectomy, I had never administered general anesthesia. Today, anesthesiology is a highly specialized field for a reason. If not handled correctly, patients can die from receiving too much of the drug or suffer great pain if not given enough. For this procedure, an orthopedic surgeon from Boston was performing the operation. I was afraid to keep the anesthesia very deep for fear of overdosing the patient, and in the middle of the procedure, the surgeon said to me, "Doctor, the patient is about to walk off the table." I increased the ether and hoped. Thankfully, all turned out well.

On October 28, 1944, I reported to the naval receiving station on Great Diamond Island in Casco Bay, Portland, Maine. The station housed sailors from the time they left their ship until they got a new assignment. My job was to take care of their medical needs, which was not difficult, since most of the men were in good health. This was also soft living: good food, drinks in the officers' club, a beautiful bay, plenty of social life on shore, and only an occasional patient or two in the sick bay.

Still, I'll never forget one of those patients, and I'm sure he remembers me to this day. A twenty-three-year-old ensign came to see me about some problems with his prepuce, the foreskin that overhangs the uncircumcised penis. He told me he had been on board a ship for several months and had recently married his long-time girlfriend. He asked me if I would circumcise him, and I agreed to do it. I gave the sailor local Novocain anesthesia and made the first incision. He screamed. I injected more anesthesia, started operating, and he screamed again. There was no stopping, so I completed the operation. Years later, it dawned on me as to why the patient was in such pain: the medical corpsman assisting me probably gave me saline solution to inject into the patient rather than Novocain. I felt terrible for the agony the patient endured. Worst of all for him, the next day, he got a two-week leave and was heading back home to see his wife.

On December 15, 1944, a month and a half after arriving at Casco Bay, I received news that would change my life forever. I had just had a pleasant date with a nurse onshore and was waiting for the boat to take me back to the island. When the boat arrived, a lieutenant commander stepped off, came over to me, and said, "Doctor, your orders just arrived at the base." When I got to the office, I read the brief document. It had been sent to me by Randall Jacobs, the chief of naval personnel in Washington, DC. The cryptic instructions stated, "You will regard yourself detached from duty at the Receiving Station, Casco Bay, Maine." Instead, I was to go to Washington "and report to the Chief of Naval Operations, Navy Department, for temporary duty, pending further assignment to duty by the Bureau of Naval Personnel."[2]

I was intrigued but also nervous. Whatever I was being asked to do had to be an important mission, or else why summon me to Washington? But I also wondered why I was being given so little information.

In early January, I spent a few days with my family in New York City. Then I headed to Washington as I was ordered to do. I had no idea what awaited me there.

5

EN ROUTE TO CHINA

In the 1940s, Chinese Nationalist forces under Chiang Kai-shek were engaged simultaneously in two conflicts in their own territory. On the one hand, they were resisting the Japanese invasion that had begun in 1937 with the notorious Rape of Nanking. Simultaneously, they were also struggling for internal control against Mao Zedong's Communists. While I was in medical school, I gave little thought to these struggles on the other side of the globe. Yet, as hard as this would have been for me to believe when I was ordered to go to Washington, DC, on that December day in 1944, I was to play a critical important role in the conflict.

After spending a few days at home in New York City, I reported to the chief of naval operations in Washington, DC, on January 9, 1945, as I had been instructed to do. I was taken into a large conference room and instructed to sit down with two officers. They could say very little about my assignment, although they did let me know it was dangerous.

"All we can tell you about your assignment is that it is voluntary," I remember one of them saying, "and that it is prolonged, extra-hazardous, overseas duty in China. You don't have to take it. If you don't, you'll be reassigned." The officers also informed me that the duty for which I was selected was connected with a secret project and that I was forbidden to discuss any details of my assignment with anyone except my supervisors. I could divulge to loved ones only that I was going to China. The officers then filled me in just a little bit more: I was going to be a part of a military partnership between China and the United States, called the Sino-American Cooperative Organization (SACO), also known as the US Naval Group, China.

I quickly thought, *I have no idea what it would be like to serve in China, but if I don't accept this assignment, I could end up landing on a beachhead somewhere in the Pacific. And China had to be an interesting place to be.* I told the officers that I'd do it.

On February 13, about a month after that initial Washington meeting, I received written orders from Chief of Naval Personnel Jacobs that I was to "proceed to the port in which the Commander, U. S. Naval Group, China, may be" with my baggage. Three other navy lieutenants were included on the orders.[1] When I arrived at the port in Washington, a large group of navy men were waiting on the sidewalk, appearing just as perplexed as I was. Some officers escorted us onto buses; after that, we headed to the railroad station and boarded a troop train. The trip took a little over a week. When we stopped at a station along the way, I slipped off the train and called my sister. Cele was also in the navy and stationed in San Diego. I asked her to meet me in Los Angeles, where our train would be stopping.

Cele was waiting on the platform. She and I had a late dinner together at a fine restaurant. We talked on and on about the past and what our futures might bring. For the first time, I learned about Cele's extraordinary military service. She had become one of six WAVES (Women Accepted for Volunteer Emergency Service), aerial navigators who trained pilots for the dangerous flights from North Island, California, naval air base to the Hawaiian Islands. These sixteen-hour flights flew at night, covering extraordinarily long distances over water and enduring headwinds that only increased the risk. Because war conditions required radio silence, the pilots had only the stars to lead them. I told Cele all the information the navy said I could disclose; that is, I was being sent to China.

LEAVING AMERICA

The next day, Cele drove me to San Pedro, location of the Los Angeles Harbor, where I and several thousand other American soldiers boarded the USS *Admiral W. S. Benson*. Most were army personnel. The only navy seamen on the ship were the crew and about ten of us SACO officers. We sailed out under a blue, Southern California sky, wondering what China would be like and what we would be doing once we got there.

Figure 5.1. *A meaningful get-together*: My sister, Cele, and I on our day together before I left for China during World War II. (Photograph courtesy of Cecilia Rosenthal.)

Just after we left shore, we got a firsthand view of war. A small plane appeared, towing a fluttering target on a cable that the navy soldiers on the ship were to shoot for practice. Gunners on deck started shooting rounds of antiaircraft missiles at the banner. We watched from the deck, in awe as one of the shots got a direct hit on the banner, and we all screamed and cheered. I was relieved to see the soldiers destroy the practice target. For the enemy, a troop ship was, in itself, a key target. It made me feel we had a chance of surviving if we were attacked.

There was much camaraderie on board, and yet I still was not fully accepted by some because I was Jewish. But I do have one fond memory of how prejudice led to friendship. One day, after we had been at sea for a couple of days, an army captain was standing with me at the railing and said, "Hank, you're a Jew, aren't you? Tell me, why is it that Jews always tried to get out of going overseas?"

"What makes you think that?" I asked.

"When our group was in camp getting ready to go overseas, there was a big line at sick bay and most of those in line were Jews," he responded. "They must have been faking illness to avoid the mission."

"How did you know they were Jews?" I questioned.

"From their names," he answered, "when the nurse called them up."

"I see," I said. "But let me ask you, how many of them were Catholics?"

"Don't know," the captain replied.

"Okay. How many were Protestants?" I demanded.

He shrugged.

"Is it possible that you're prejudiced, and that every time they called a Jewish name, you were conscious of it, but you didn't consider the religion of the other people called?" I asked.

"You know, you're right," he conceded.

"I'll tell you what," I said to him. "Why don't you come with me to the Friday night Jewish services on the ship, and we'll see how many Jewish men there are?" The man agreed to go.

I had no idea just how many Jews would be at the services, but I had already thrown down the gauntlet at that point. Still, I was vindicated. When Friday night arrived, the man and I went to the dining hall where Jewish services were held. We saw several hundred soldiers and sailors in attendance. After that, the captain and I were friends for the rest of the trip. I had gained his respect for my taking a stand, and he had gained my respect for being open to learning.

On March 29, 1945, after we had been at sea for thirty-two days, we landed in Bombay (now known as Mumbai), India. Four days later, we boarded a train to Calcutta (also known as Kolkata). Two officers and I shared a comfortable, screened, private room with its own lavatory, while the enlisted men lived in second-class cars that were open on both sides with long wooden benches shared for sitting and sleeping. The train was pulled by an ancient steam engine. Sometimes it stopped because a cow, deemed holy according to the Hindu religion, was standing on the track. At these interludes, we would take our aluminum canteen cups and hike forward to the engine. As we held the cup under the exhaust, the engineer ejected steam into the cup, providing hot, sterile water for making coffee.

After four days on the train, we reached Calcutta and were driven to Kanchrapara, a US Army camp. I still had no idea how I was getting to China or what I would be doing. The dirt roads to the camp were narrow and always lined with people carrying heavy loads attached to poles or atop their heads. One evening in the officer's club, I heard an American laughing. "I knocked off two gooks with my truck today," he said, meaning that he had run over two Indian locals. The remark sickened me. I had grown a stiff hatred for Nazis, but I suddenly realized that anyone who hates others in a prejudicial way could be found in any country, including the United States.

Later that night, a few of us went walking and saw a small, attractive building surrounded by beautiful gardens. On the gate was a bronze plaque with the name "Punjab Club." We wandered in and were met at the door by a young Indian officer who cordially invited us inside. There were other Indian soldiers there, pleasant and bright men who welcomed us with food and friendship. One soldier asked a question that made us laugh: "Is America going to take India from the British after the war?" We assured them that we would not. I thought about the Indians' hospitality and warmth and questioned, "Who among us are really the 'gooks'?"

I AM A MULE FOR THE US NAVY

On April 18, 1945, I received orders telling me to board a commercial aircraft that would fly me to Chungking, China. There, I would report to the office SACO's commander, Milton E. Miles. I was given a civilian American passport and was required to wear civilian khakis without any insignia rather than wear my uniform. The idea was to blend in with the other passengers aboard the plane and not to tip anyone off that I was in the military. I soon found out that I was to be a short-term "mule" for the American government, delivering supplies to the Americans in China, although I still did not know just where in the country that would be.

I was given five huge mail pouches and a letter marked "Secret." In the pouches were mail, rifles, and ammunition. In addition, I was loaded down with a half dozen .45-caliber pistols hanging from straps over my shoulders and in holsters on my belt. The pilot didn't want me to board the small plane because it was too much weight. He worked for the government-controlled Chinese National Aviation Corporation, or CNAC, which owned the plane. But the man who accompanied me, who worked for the US embassy, popped his head in and told the pilot that I was part of an important military mission. We took off at 0400.

The "commercial aircraft" in which we flew to Chungking was a two-engine passenger plane, a C47 cast off by the US Air Force to the CNAC. The plane ascended rapidly and we headed over the Hump, a pass from India to China through the Himalayas. We had to climb to more than seventeen thousand feet to get over the mountains. There were holes in the windows through which we could fire a gun if attacked by a Japanese plane. I later learned that that was not unusual.

As the air grew thinner and thinner, I began gasping for breath. This became increasingly painful, relieved only when I lost consciousness, as we all did. Only the pilot and copilot had oxygen masks. I have no idea how long we lived with limited oxygen. The next thing I remember, my eyes suddenly popped open, and I was wide-awake. I looked out the window and saw row after row of rice paddies all around the sides of the hills. We were in China.

The plane landed in Chungking, China's wartime capital. The "airport" was a small sand island in the Yangtze River. Upon landing, I got into a bamboo chair and lay back as two coolies (working-class Chinese), one in front and the other in back, carried me on their shoulders up steep and lengthy stone stairs leading from the river bed to street level. My five mailbags were also hauled up on the backs of coolies. When the coolies set me down, no one was there to meet me, so I stood in the street for quite a while. After an hour or so, a jeep pulled up and drove me to SACO headquarters.

MY MISSION DISCLOSED

The next day, I met in a small room with two US Navy officers who finally revealed to me the details of my assignment and explained a bit more about SACO's mission.

The organization was formed in 1943 as a top-secret military partnership between the government of Chiang Kai-shek and the government of the United States to help defeat Japan. Having received direct funding from President Franklin D. Roosevelt's office, SACO gathered key intelligence from China and communicated it to Washington.

The need for such intelligence was heightened after the Japanese brutally took Nanking. Commander Miles was once again sent to Chungking in western China, and the country became a patchwork of tenuous loyalties with nationalists, Communists, the Japanese, Chinese puppet generals, and assorted independent warlords all jockeying for dominance in this tumultuous area.

Miles was advised specifically to have no communication with a particularly powerful and brutal Chinese warlord named Lieutenant General Tai Li. He was Chiang Kai-shek's powerful head of the secret police who "recruited" villagers at bayonet point to join his guerrilla army. His mission was to protect China from the dual threat of foreign imperialism and homegrown Communism. Tai Li ruthlessly carried out Chiang Kai-shek's instructions, eliminating political opposition and reserving for himself the fruits of illegal smuggling operations.

Miles needed accurate intelligence gathering regarding Japanese fleet movements, but he was getting nowhere with his mission of setting up US naval bases on the Chinese coast. Then he received an interesting invitation from none other than Tai Li. He offered to take Miles on a trip through Japanese-occupied China to demonstrate that the Chinese general had access to all areas of his country due to his tight control of the police. With Miles dressed in Chinese clothes, the two traveled relatively safely down the Yangtze River on a *sampan*, a flat-bottomed, wooden boat. They visited Shanghai and other Japanese-occupied territories. The men formed a firm relationship, and, on July 4, 1943, they signed the SACO treaty.

With this partnership in place, the United States could set up camps in the interior of China and report on weather conditions originating there, specifically in the far-west region of the country. These weather reports then would be radioed to headquarters in Chungking. Knowing the conditions was valuable in that it could help predict weather in the Pacific Ocean, where the US Pacific Fleet operated, three weeks in advance. US Navy and US Marine personnel set up and monitored weather stations in the Gobi Desert in Inner Mongolia. In eastern China, a network of coast watchers reported Japanese fleet movements. For example, SACO coast watchers in Shanghai frequently radioed to US submarines when a Japanese ship was leaving the dock so the Americans could intercept the ships at sea with torpedoes.

And just what did Tai Li get out of the deal? He needed to strengthen his guerrilla forces to be ready to fight the Japanese, so US sailors and marines trained his Chinese soldiers in combat and in other areas. All told, SACO established a network of over a dozen guerrilla-training posts, many of them doubling as weather stations, throughout China.

And that's where I came in. I was sent to US Naval Unit Four, the one located in Inner Mongolia, which was known as Camp Four. In addition to training Chinese soldiers, Camp Four was to maintain a hospital facility behind Japanese lines not far from the coast. The clinic would serve the Allied forces that were expected to soon land in China as part of a plan to invade Japan.

I had no way of knowing then just how the time I would spend at Camp Four would influence my worldview and the way I practiced medicine throughout my career.

ARRIVAL IN CHINA

Set squarely on the edge of the Gobi Desert, Camp Four was the most remote American-backed clandestine military-training base in China. It was strategically located in the Gobi Desert to support the army of a general named Fu Tso Yi. He was a powerful military leader. During the summer of 1945, the main obstacle that stood in the way of a Japanese attack on Camp Four was the presence of a nationalist Chinese army, one hundred thousand men strong, under Fu's command.

The day after arriving in Chungking, I ran a fever of 104 degrees and was about to collapse. The headquarters physician examined me. The diagnosis was bacillary dysentery and they immediately put me to bed in the sick bay. The vomiting and diarrhea lasted three days. Despite my suffering, I received orders to proceed to Camp Four. I was going to the Gobi Desert, regardless of my physical condition. But it was also a psychological challenge: I was a kid from New Rochelle who was going to live on the opposite side of the world from where I had been my whole life, and I had no idea how long I would be there.

And yet, I had to chuckle. All along, the sea-lover in me had joined the navy to sail the high seas, and here I was, about to head to just about the driest place on earth.

I was flown to Lanchow, an ancient city in Kansu Province and the gateway to the West for Chinese traders, as it had been since the days of Marco Polo. There, I was met by a US Navy lieutenant commander and three enlisted weathermen with whom I was to travel north. The lieutenant commander and one weatherman were going northwest to Tsinjiang to set up a weather station. Traveling in the back of a truck, we made our way over well-groomed, sandy roads to a walled-in city and dropped off two weathermen there. Next, we headed toward the city of Ningsia in Ningsia Province, after which time they would drop me off and I would head to Inner Mongolia.

The warlord Ma Hongkui, known as General Ma, controlled the mostly Muslim Ningsia Province. General Ma arranged for our accommodations, and we were put up in grand style for a week. After having been on the road for several weeks, we were grateful to have excellent food, showers, and a clean bed. Wherever we went, we rode in Ma's colonial-style carriages drawn by horses, similar to those in New York City's Central Park. As General Ma rode in his carriage, a half dozen soldiers carrying submachine guns ran alongside.

Figure 5.2. *A prominent family*: General Ma of Ningsia Province treated us navy men well.

After a week, a truck from Camp Four arrived to pick me up. We left the comforts of Ningsia, heading north, and were ferried across the Huang Po (or Yellow Bank River). We continued on a hardened-dirt road, marked only by the tire tracks of trucks that had preceded us, toward the town of Shanpa, the capital of Suiyuan Province. The land was looking more desolate. A few trees and mud homes dotted the sandy landscape. We passed through the collection of one-story, dun-colored adobe buildings that was Shanpa.

Small and nondescript as it was, Shanpa was a regional stronghold for Chinese nationalists. Fifty miles to the east were tens of thousands of Japanese troops, as well as Chinese military puppets, which were Chinese armies that had gone over to the Japanese side during the nine years Japan had controlled

China. Thirty miles north of the region were more puppets, more Japanese, and an Imperial Japanese intelligence office. It was not difficult to understand why this was an "extra hazardous" duty; Japanese forces were nearly all around us.

Figure 5.3. *Getting to know a strange country*: I had this photo of me taken in front of a Chinese temple.

We headed west out of Shanpa, and about ten miles later, we finally reached Camp Four. It was June 4, 1945. It had been nearly four months since I'd left Washington, DC.

6

A HEALTH CLINIC IN
THE GOBI DESERT

Camp Four was surrounded by huge waves of white sand that extended as far as the eye could see. In the distance, in a haze, was the mountain range the local people called the Big Blue Mountains. As we approached Camp Four, we could see tents pitched as barracks for Chinese soldiers, guerrillas who were being trained by the US Marines stationed there. High, mud walls surrounded the camp; on the walls were painted foot-high Chinese characters praising the "Nationalist cause." Two Chinese sentries holding American rifles flanked the gate and waved us in.

Figure 6.1. *Working together*: Those of us stationed at Camp Four relied on a Chinese guerrilla army for protection from Japanese forces and Chinese Communist rogue forces nearby.

Our quarters at Camp Four had once been a Belgian Catholic mission. The buildings had glass windows, unlike all other buildings in that part of China, which had rice-paper-covered window openings. Most of the men's beds were made with wooden frames and crisscrossed rope on which they placed their sleeping bags. I slept in a sleeping bag on a clay platform known as a *kang*. We had Chinese interpreters available, and every American had a houseboy to make the beds, clean up, and bring hot water for washing.

I was one of twelve Americans stationed at Camp Four—six navy men and six marines working under the navy. "The Apostles" was our code name. I replaced another doctor who had to leave to get back to headquarters in Chungking for dental work. The main part of my job was to provide medical care to our American men, as well as to Chinese soldiers and the local villagers.

Figure 6.2. *A powerful warlord*: Keeping General Fu Tso Yi on the side of the United States was critical to maintaining a stronghold in China.

The man responsible for our accommodations and just about everything else in the camp was General Fu Tso Yi. General Fu had provided each American at Camp Four with a Mongolian pony for transportation. Getting around on a small Chinese horse was certainly not a customary activity for a young man from New York City. My first time getting on the animal was a complete disaster. The horse shied at a piece of paper blowing on the road, and it threw me over its head. After a few weeks, however, I was riding as well as anyone, galloping through dried-up irrigation ditches and racing my friends.

General Fu's influence extended beyond Camp Four and into the surrounding region. Fu was loyal to Chiang Kai-shek and opposed the Japanese, as well as the rogue Chinese Communist forces in the area. But US officials were not sure how long his loyalty would last. Many other Chinese military leaders had become puppets of the Japanese. The reason I was there, and the doctors before me, was to appease Fu. If we provided medical care to the local people and kept on good terms with them, the US believed it would increase the likelihood that Fu's nationalist army—one hundred thousand men strong—would remain on our side against the Japanese and keep nearby rogue Communist Chinese forces at bay.

Figure 6.3. *A New Yorker in the desert*: When I joined the navy, I had no idea I would serve in the deserts of Inner Mongolia.

SETTING UP A MEDICAL CLINIC

There wasn't much of a medical clinic at Camp Four when I got there. There was no place to operate and no ready supply of sanitized water. The water came from an open well used by anyone passing by, including camel caravans. The roiling winds of the Mongolian plateau left the well water contaminated with dirt and animal dung. Camp latrines were simply holes dug in the ground, which attracted disease-bearing flies. The doctor who had been there before I arrived and the one before him were not surgeons, and they treated patients only on an occasional basis. The camp's ample supply of surgical instruments and medication were packed away in boxes.

I figured I would make changes to the camp so that we could treat more patients under better conditions. First on the list was setting up a rudimentary operating room that was as sanitary as possible. To clean up the water supply, I had some of the Chinese men build a wall around the cesspool and protect it with a wooden cover. Then we rigged up a hinged pole device that would lower a bucket into the well to retrieve clean water. I had the men build a wall around the latrine holes, which they covered after partially filling them with lime.

Then I turned to surgical preparations. We had some surgical instruments, materials for bandaging up patients, and a small amount of antibiotics and other drugs. What we didn't have was a system to sterilize water, so I engineered one. We commandeered a kettle, stuck copper tubing through a cork on its spout, and twisted it around in a spiral pattern upward and then downward so that steam condensed within it and dripped into a bottle sterilized in boiling water. Next, using a five-gallon oil drum with a tight-fitting lid and a wooden platform that we fitted inside the oil drum a few inches from the bottom, we made a field-hospital "sterilizer." We filled the space under the platform with water, placed sheets on the platform, corked the top tightly, and put the contraption on hot coals, our serviceable steam-pressure "autoclave." Finally, I had the Shanpa coffin maker build me an operating table. Following a sketch I gave him, he constructed a sturdy wooden table with a hinged, adjustable head and leg pieces. Once finished, he delivered it by donkey wagon to Camp Four.

These preparations were completed none too soon. Barely two weeks after my arrival, I stepped away from the wooden operating table, looked out of the mud-walled operating room, and gazed across the sands of the Gobi desert. In the fading light of dusk, I saw a middle-aged Chinese man approaching the camp. He was bent over, carrying a young girl on his back. I had no idea how far he had come with her.

She was his daughter, the peasant told my interpreter. "Bu whei cher fan," the man said sorrowfully. *She cannot eat.* He said she had been vomiting for the past two weeks. He brought the girl into the makeshift operating room and I examined her. She was about eighteen years old, severely dehydrated, and barely conscious. Her abdomen was hugely swollen. Was it a tumor or an infection? With only a nine-month surgical internship at Boston City Hospital, I wasn't certain of the answer.

I could see that she would die if left untreated, and so I decided I would have to operate to figure out what was wrong. It was nearly nightfall, however, and since we had no electric lights, it would be foolhardy to begin an operation this close to dark. Instead, I treated the dehydration immediately and planned to operate in the morning. I added salt tablets to condensed steam from our "still" and injected the saline solution under her skin. I didn't want to risk an intravenous injection because, in these circumstances, the sterility of the solution couldn't be guaranteed, and that could destroy her red blood cells.

It was all I could do until daylight, so I went to get some sleep. Before I did that, however, I had the corpsman sterilize some instruments in boiling water and ready some sheets from the oil-drum autoclave. I also told the father that if his daughter made it through the night, I would operate. The girl and her father spent the night in a spare room in our compound. I must admit that I had to consider letting her die rather than operate in view of my minimal surgical experience and the primitive surgical equipment. The Chinese villagers already distrusted Western medicine, perceiving us doctors as foreign devils. If the young woman died during or after surgery, the Chinese living in the area would refuse to come for medical care. We would lose face as a medical unit and would probably have to leave.

The next morning, thanks to the saline infusion, my patient was somewhat improved. Adjusting the coffin maker's table, I gave the girl a spinal anesthesia, and we set to work. I painted the girl's abdomen with iodine and placed the sterilized drape over her. Then I carefully cut through the skin into the abdominal cavity.

When I hit the peritoneum, the abdominal lining, something amazing happened. Green and yellow pus gushed out of the incision, soaking me and the assisting corpsman standing nearby. I screamed with delight, eliciting a glance of considerable amazement from the corpsman. This meant that the cause of the patient's distress was an infection, a huge pelvic abscess. I was joyful because I knew I could handle an infection. At Boston City Hospital, draining even a massive abscess like this one would have been considered a fairly routine procedure—although I personally had never done such an operation before. Had she had a tumor, I would not have known what to do.

I cleaned out the abscess, inserted rubber tubing to drain the infection, and left the wound partially open to continue the drainage process. We monitored her carefully, and, bit by bit, her color and spirits returned. About a week later, the girl was well enough to travel.

"Hsie hsie, mei gwa daifu," her father said, bowing, as they left. *Thank you, American doctor.*

GENERAL FU TSO YI

Word of the girl's recovery spread in Shanpa and throughout the countryside. Many saw it as a miracle. Those who had seen the girl before the operation expected her to die, and when she went home smiling a week later, my stock as a physician shot up dramatically. It seemed as if the entire scattered population of the region was suddenly converging on Camp Four. First in a trickle and soon in a stream, people who had never before had contact with Western medicine began to knock on the door of my little "clinic." They came on foot or by horse. The wealthier ones were carried in sedan chairs. A few were so sick, they crawled in. For some, the trip had taken them many days. All wanted to be treated by the *mei gwa daifu*, the "doctor from the beautiful country, America."

Most notably, news of the girl's survival reached the ears of General Fu Tso Yi, the warlord whom we wanted to remain loyal to Chiang Kai-shek.

A few days after I treated the girl for her pelvic abscess, a Chinese soldier drove into the camp. He explained through our interpreter that General Fu wanted to see me, and we sped off in his jeep to Fu's barracks about thirty miles away. As I sat down in Fu's office, the general seemed stiff and formal. He and his senior staff dressed in full uniform. But as we began to talk, he relaxed and appeared pleasant and appreciative. That's when I came up with an idea to satisfy my secondary mission—that is, to retain Fu's loyalty.

Through the interpreter, who spoke to Fu in Mandarin, I proposed an idea that had never been done before: we could develop a medical corps within Fu's army that I would train. Fu liked the idea and ordered that I be given his best soldiers. Within a short time, twenty-five of Fu's men were bandaging wounds and learning basic diagnostics and routine care under my supervision.

I was now equipped with my own two American medical corpsmen and a small but eager contingent of Chinese soldiers.

AN INNOVATION IN THE DESERT

I needed all the help I could get. In subsequent weeks at Camp Four, I saw illnesses that were far more advanced than they would have ever progressed in the West and an array of ailments that had been virtually eliminated back home. Some conditions, such as scurvy, were due to a simple lack of proper nutrients, in which case, all that was needed was a regimen of vitamin C. But there were also patients suffering from pneumonic and bubonic plagues because the nearby Japanese army had driven the rats that carried plague fleas out of the areas they controlled and into ours. I saw many cases of advanced syphilis and some cases of smallpox. One man was brought to me with what my interpreter called a "sore throat" only to discover that a syphilitic gumma, an ulceration, had eaten a large hole in the roof of his mouth. We treated these individuals as best we could, but without adequate medical supplies, we simply had to turn some away. For the most part, though, I was able to treat the locals' illnesses with either vitamins, drugs, or surgery.

Figure 6.4. *Helping the locals*: After word spread that I had saved the life of a villager, people traveled long distances to be treated by this new, Western doctor.

One problem, however, had me stymied. It was a debilitating eye disease that caused blindness if left untreated. My dog-eared medical books called it trachoma, and it was rampant throughout Asia and Africa. As it turned out, a drug called sulfanilamide recently had been found to be effective in treating trachoma, but stationed where I was, I had no way of knowing that.

Trachoma is caused by bacteria carried by flies—flies that have an affinity for people's eyes. When a trachoma-carrying fly lands on someone's eyelids, the microbe incites an inflammation that scars the lids and curls them inward, causing the eyelashes, in turn, to scratch the cornea. After a period of years, this chronic irritation usually results in scarring of the cornea, leading to blindness.

From the moment I encountered my first case of trachoma, I couldn't get the problem out of my mind. I began to ponder drugs that had been found to be effective against other infections. One antimicrobial agent I was aware of was sulfadiazine, so it seemed logical to give it a try. The good news was that we had a fair amount of sulfa on hand. The bad news was that the drug was available only in tablet form. Taking sulfa by mouth requires a higher dose than if the infection is treated topically, and I didn't want to run out of it. Plus, applying the treatment topically is more effective than if the patient swallows tablets.

I was confounded by the challenge of figuring out how to apply the tablets directly to the eye. This problem brewed in my mind for two or three days until I suddenly thought of a possible solution. The Camp Four commissary didn't have eye ointment, but it did have an ample supply of Barbasol shaving cream. This was the pre-aerosol era, when shaving cream came in squeeze tubes, like toothpaste. I had no idea if this admittedly unorthodox treatment would work, but I did know that it would not injure the eye. Furthermore, shaving cream was smooth, so it could act as a binding agent. Besides, it was all we had. The only downside, I thought, was that it would probably cause stinging, as Barbasol is basically a soap.

I had a navy corpsman grind up sulfadiazine tablets into a fine powder. I squeezed out a few tubes of shaving cream, mixed the powder into it, and looked around for some initial test subjects. General Fu obligingly "volunteered" several of his trachoma-afflicted soldiers, and one bright afternoon, they trooped into Camp Four, reporting for duty as ordered to the *mei gwa daifu*. Since there were no chairs available, I asked them, one by one, to lie on their backs on the ground. Then I dipped a small, sterilized stick into the sulfa-and-Barbasol mixture and dabbed it carefully into the edge of each soldier's eyelids.

The treatment was no picnic for the soldiers; they moaned and groaned, twisting on the ground as if they had been stabbed in the eyes. This continued for some time, and we had a tussle or two, convincing the young men not to wipe the ointment away. I repeated several more treatments a few days apart. As I had hoped, the drug began to work. The soldiers' trachoma cleared up, and the eyelid inflammation healed. Using this primitive cure, we had triumphed in beating an epidemic disease, one that no one in China—or as far as I knew, the rest of the world—had previously solved.

Figure 6.5. *My first medical innovation*: When I saw how trachoma was causing many Chinese to go blind, I whipped up an antidote of sulfa and shaving cream.

News of the soap-and-sulfa cure traveled fast, and people again swarmed my clinic—but this time, the clinic was filled with individuals who suffered from trachoma. I soon began a strange, daily routine: First thing in the morning, fifty or sixty trachoma-infected locals, townspeople, and even soldiers showed up at the door of my clinic. By this point, I had trained my Chinese corpsmen in applying the ointment, and we treated the new arrivals as I had treated the first round of Fu's soldiers. For the next fifteen or twenty minutes, dozens of patients squirmed and screamed on the ground in agony. Then they would leave, and the same madhouse scene would be repeated the following day.

A few months later, after the war ended, our first mail arrived. I read a notice in an armed-forces medical journal that other doctors in other parts of the world had also discovered the sulfadiazine cure for trachoma. It was gratifying to find that my first "research" had been independently confirmed— although, as far as I recall, I was the only one to have to resort to using shaving cream!

A PATIENT DIES

My medical challenges at Camp Four continued, but there was one incident in particular that has stayed with me even to this day.

On August 15, 1945, the war officially ended with the surrender of Japan. We Apostles waited with anticipation for our orders to leave Camp Four and return home. But we received no word from the navy. It was a precarious and dangerous time. Without the Japanese in the picture, we knew, with terrible foreboding, that a conflagration between Chiang's and Mao's forces was just around the corner and that General Fu would be one of the leaders of the conflict. Without orders to leave, we wondered if the navy was intentionally keeping us there to be used as pawns. Had we become casualties, it would have given the military a prime excuse to enter the developing civil war and try to defeat the Communists.

One day, about two months after the war ended, I was sitting in my dispensary. It was not much past dawn. I could hear the guerrillas' guns firing in the distance as they practiced their marksmanship. I had become used to those drills, as the men were in a constant state of readiness in anticipation of the domestic upheaval that might begin at any minute. I hardly noticed when the firing ceased, an indication that something terrible had happened. Then one of the interpreters ran in.

"A man's been shot!" he yelled. "They're bringing him here."

In a few minutes, two Chinese soldiers lumbered in, carrying in their arms the blood-covered body of a third soldier. The victim was a young man who had been riding his horse in formation with other guerrillas when a fellow soldier's gun accidentally fired, shooting a bullet into his companion's back. The bullet traveled straight through his body and out through his chest.

The wound was terrible, a raw gash five or six inches in length, shattering flesh and bone and tearing into the young man's lungs. In those days, even at Boston City Hospital, where I'd done my brief surgical internship, chest surgery was still in its infancy. I had never seen or heard of a surgeon who had opened a chest before.

I did the best I knew how to do. First, I sutured one of his torn lungs and tried to close the cavity. But the damage was massive, and with the limited equipment available, I could not find a way to properly drain the chest cavity. This was critical, because it would have relieved a life-threatening pressure of air and blood pushing down on the man's lungs. There was no way to control the bleeding. As I closed up the wound, the soldier died.

Physicians always recall the first patient who dies in their care, and the memory of the Chinese soldier who died on my operating table at Camp Four in 1945 tore me up. Afterward, I got on my horse and headed into town to have dinner. I just wanted some time to be alone. When I got halfway between the camp and the town, I wearily scanned the gray expanses, and my eyes picked up an oxcart on the eastern horizon heading across the fields, moving away from me. As I drew closer, I could make out a man walking alongside a cart that was jostling and bouncing as the wooden wheels caught ruts in the field. There was a coffin in the cart. A lump stuck in my throat as I realized that it held the body of the young man who had died in my hands that afternoon.

I never forgot the sight of the soldier's coffin and vowed that, one day, I would make amends to him.

TRANSPORTING A KILLER

On October 29, 1945, we were finally given our orders that we would be transported back to the United States. Our struggle to treat patients under base conditions in the middle of the Gobi Desert was over. No longer did I have to think of diplomatic ways to appease Chinese military leaders. Yet it would be seven months before I was again able to feel American ground under my feet.

I spent several months stationed on a ship in Shanghai, where I treated US soldiers. One day, a commanding officer summoned me to his office to tell me that I was to work on a landing craft used to transport prisoners from Japan. I knew the conditions on that particular ship were abysmal. Because the prisoners were not given proper facilities, the ship stunk of excrement and urine. After having been in Inner Mongolia, I had lost forty-five pounds and developed dysentery. I didn't think I could last living in those conditions.

After the commander gave me the news, I pointed through the porthole to a hospital ship that was docked.

"Commander, see that hospital ship? I've been in the interior of China in a guerrilla army for months. You have a choice. You can send me there as a doctor or as a patient."

I must have been convincing, because I soon received orders to be transferred to the hospital ship, the USS *Repose* (AH-16). The *Repose* was a beautiful, fully equipped, 400-bed facility. Its only action was to deliver female nurses to the Pacific as the war ended. There was a lot of partying, and the ship was brilliantly lit up at night. (It was said that no crewmember actually slept on the *Repose*, at least alone.)

Living on the hospital ship was a great experience. I led the ship's band, and we played jazz on the deck. But I still had my medical duties. I treated men with serious conditions. Some died from infectious diseases. In one case, a man arrived from China on a stretcher and was foaming at the mouth. The ship's medical crew was puzzled about his condition, but I had seen similar cases before in China. "This man has pneumonic plague and will be dead in less than an hour," I told them. The man, indeed, died as I had predicted. Later, a smear of his saliva examined under a microscope was found to have plague bacteria.

My ticket home came one night in April of 1946, when a US Navy sailor was carried aboard the *Repose* on a stretcher, a victim of a stab wound to the belly. I soon learned that the wound was self-inflicted and that the man had murdered nine of his fellow soldiers.

Earlier that night, nineteen-year-old Seaman Second Class William Vincent Smith had come off guard duty of his ship and went to his bunk, carrying a rifle and wearing a revolver and a sheath knife. The ship's men were asleep in their bunks, which lined the bulkhead. Smith sat on his own bunk, aimed his rifle, and began picking off his sailor mates, one by one, as they slept. Sailors who awakened came after Smith, but he shot them with his pistol. Then Smith stabbed himself in the abdomen with his sheath knife. He had shot ten men; nine died immediately. I never learned if the tenth man survived.[1]

I operated on Smith's knife wound. Although the knife had deeply penetrated his abdomen, it had missed internal organs, so I only had to sew the incision closed. Smith was placed in a lock ward where he was guarded at all times. I occasionally visited Smith to change his dressing and asked him if he felt what he had done was wrong. He said no. "My father took me hunting when I was small and we shot squirrels. I don't see any difference," he said matter-of-factly. A number of psychiatrists were brought in from the States to evaluate Smith, but none would make a decision as to whether he was sane enough to be tried for the murders.

While Smith sat in his holding cell, recovering from his injuries, I finally received the news I was waiting for. On May 18, 1946, not quite a year and a half after I had left the United States, my commanding officer told me that I could leave for home the next day. There was just one catch: I would be taking Smith with me.

It was a top-secret trip because word was out that friends of Smith's victims were planning to kill him. I knew that if anything happened to Smith while he was in my care, I could be court-martialed. But I didn't worry too much about that. I was going home.

An ambulance took Smith, four hospital corpsmen, and me to the Shanghai airport. Smith wore a straightjacket and was tied to a wire-mesh stretcher. We boarded a C-46 plane and landed in a navy base on the island of Guam. Smith was placed in a locked cell, still wearing his straightjacket. While we waited for further orders, a navy psychiatrist from New York City took me in hand and showed me around the area. We swam on beautiful beaches and had our meals in the officer's club.

But while we were enjoying ourselves, I began to feel anxious about my mission, about getting Smith to the United States. A few days after arriving in Guam, I wrote a memo to the admiral in charge, stating that we should leave immediately. The next day, the admiral called me in and gave me some shocking news: The psychiatrist who had taken me around and acted so friendly had apparently been telling officers that he was worried about my mental state. He then suggested that he, rather than I, take Smith to the United States. Fortunately, the admiral disagreed with the psychiatrist's recommendation and let me leave with Smith the next day, along with a small group of corpsmen. On May 25, I delivered Smith to a navy hospital on Mare Island, off the coast of California. In August of 1947, I read in the newspaper that Smith had hung himself and died in jail while awaiting a court martial.[2] On June 18, I arrived in New York City to a wonderful homecoming.

On July 1, 1946, I was given my US Navy discharge papers and assigned to the US Navy Reserves.

I look back on my time serving as a military doctor in China as one of the most challenging and rewarding times of my life. That war-torn, impoverished, and remote part of the world certainly provided a most interesting location in which to practice medicine. Apparently, Hollywood agreed, for in 1953, Twentieth Century Fox released a dramatic movie about Camp Four. *Destination Gobi*, starring Richard Widmark, told the story of US Navy weathermen who teamed up with Chinese Mongol nomads to fight the Japanese. The film was not completely fictionalized: United States soldiers in the camp were protected from the Japanese by Chinese guerrillas—250 of them—who lived in makeshift barracks just outside the walls of Camp Four.[3]

But, as my wartime service drew to a close and I was back with my parents in New York City, it was time to move on. And so I began to fulfill my life-long dream of becoming an accomplished surgeon.

Figure 6.6. *The* Repose: I spent six months on this ship, the *Repose*, after the war ended.

7

A MEDICAL NEWBIE SEARCHES
FOR A SURGICAL RESIDENCY

By the summer of 1946, I was back in New York, a civilian, ready to find work as a resident in surgery. Surgery naturally fit with my character. I like to fix problems, and as I had learned in China, every surgical situation presented a new set of challenges, new puzzles to solve. I appreciated surgery's demand for delicacy and precision.

At the time, one of the newest fields was thoracic (or chest) surgery. This excited me. But I soon learned that obtaining a surgical residency in postwar America would not be easy. I dropped into several hospitals to inquire about positions only to be received by the surgery-department secretaries who uttered the same response: "Doctor, fifty thousand physicians have returned from the war. We have to take those who were on staff here before they went into the service." Every doctor slightly older than I was, who had exited the armed forces a year or more before I had, had grabbed the available residencies. I could have looked for jobs outside New York, but I wanted to stay close to my parents. I was further limited by anti-Semitism. In the mid-1940s, the only hospitals that were not reluctant to hire Jewish physicians were Jewish hospitals.

I inquired at a handful of hospitals and, one by one, each turned me down. However, one visit to a physician's office gave me hope. He was the chief of surgery of Lenox Hill Hospital, and I had made an appointment to see him at his private practice on Park Avenue. I got there on time for my appointment but waited a long time before his secretary admitted me to see him, even though there were no patients in the office. When I entered his office, he criticized me for being late.

"No sir, I was here early," I corrected him.

He immediately called in his secretary and quietly said, "You know you're not to keep a doctor waiting." For the first time since my return, I felt someone had treated me with respect.

After that exchange, the man recited the routine statement about the surplus of fifty thousand doctors who, like me, were getting out of the service and seeking positions.

"I'll know better next war," I said.

"Please, doctor, don't get discouraged," he said. "I understand your feelings, but I know you have ability and will turn out fine."

The surgeon's words of comfort were the first I had heard since I began looking for a residency, and I never forgot him. Decades later, after he retired, I met that doctor at a surgical conference. I had become quite well known by that time. I went up to him and reminded him of the incident of my residency days and how much his support had meant to me. He smiled, we shook hands, and he said, "I knew you would do well."

I soon was offered a position, but it was not as a surgical resident. Instead, a doctor who was an internist had offered to take me into his office, after which I would pursue board certification in internal medicine. I had a hard time deciding whether I should take the position. On the one hand, I knew I wanted to be a surgeon, but I was so discouraged by having been rejected so many times by surgeons refusing to hire me that I wondered if I should settle and accept the internist's offer.

I decided I would try one more time to get a surgical residency. This time, I applied at the most prominent Jewish hospital in New York City, Mount Sinai Hospital. Usually, I mailed in my job applications, but this time, I decided to deliver the application personally. I walked across Central Park to Mount Sinai. I asked for the office of the director of medical education and was sent there. The secretary was busy typing. I let her know I had an application to give the director.

Her eyes remained fixated on her Smith Corona. "Leave it on my desk. I'll turn it in," she said.

"I'd like to hand my application to the director personally," I told her.

"He's very busy," she said. "He's got an important meeting."

"I'll just sit in the hall and wait," I replied pleasantly and sat down.

After about fifteen minutes, the door to the director's office opened and he emerged. I stood up, blocking his exit. I let him know that I had served in the war as a physician and was seeking a surgical residency.

He began to deliver the same line I had heard from so many other physicians, how many other doctors had also gotten out of the service and were also looking for residencies.

But I stopped him before he could get all the words out, and politely—but firmly—I replied, "Please don't tell me I can't get a position because the competition is tough. I want you to tell me whether I'm good enough to be a surgeon." He stood stock-still. "Come into my office," he said.

We sat down. The director asked me about my medical training and military experience. I told him about my time running the medical unit in China.

He looked at me earnestly. "Dr. Heimlich, a patient has tenderness and pain over the right upper abdomen and is coughing up blood. What does he have?"

"Liver flukes," I answered, without missing a beat, speaking about parasites that burrow through the diaphragm and into the lung.

He smiled and then told me that he was originally from the Netherlands, where, for twenty years, he had taught and researched bone disease. He had come to America in 1938 and soon thereafter worked as a professor of medicine at the Peiping Union Medical College in Peking, China. He asked me many questions about my experiences in China, and we talked for a long time.

"What will you do if you don't get a surgical residency?" he asked me. I told him about the internist's offer.

"If you don't go into surgery, you'll never be happy," he said.

"Yes, but I can't spend the rest of my life doing nothing while waiting for a surgical residency," I said.

"Dr. Heimlich, promise me that you won't take the job with the internist until you hear from me," he said. "Give me two weeks, all right?"

I promised that I would. A week later, a letter arrived offering me a one-year surgical residency at Mount Sinai Hospital in the fall. It was the best news I could have hoped for.

A REAL EDUCATION

The one-year residency program at Mount Sinai was preceded by a six-month review course at Columbia University College of Medicine, which was designed to bring those of us who had not had formal medical training while in the armed forces up to date on what had progressed in medicine during our absence. I learned about penicillin (which had just burst on the scene), new developments in surgery, and new ways to treat burns. I had expected the course to be useless for me—I had not been away from medicine that long—but I was wrong. It was an excellent review, and I met doctors with whom I would be working at Mount Sinai, and we became friends. Overall, it was a good way to get my feet on the ground as I got back into medicine.

In July 1947, I moved into the residents' quarters at Mount Sinai Hospital, was assigned to a surgical team, and went to work. The hospital paid no salary, but I had a small income from the GI Bill of Rights and some money saved from my navy salary. And there was a side benefit: residents didn't eat in a cafeteria; we ate in a dining room with excellent food that was served by waiters.

Residents at Mount Sinai were involved only in the care of privately paying patients; we never performed operations ourselves. These patients could select their surgeons and were given private or semiprivate rooms. My goal for the future was to obtain another year's residency on the ward service, where patients received their care free of charge. These patients stayed in large rooms, separated by gender, holding thirty to fifty patients each, affording them no privacy. Furthermore, the patients had no choice of who their surgeons would be. Here, residents could operate on and care for patients under the supervision of a staff surgeon.

But in my first year, I could only assist in operations. We residents were on call every morning; during this time, we made rounds in our assigned teams, checking on patients. We broke for lunch, assisted in surgery through the afternoon, broke for dinner, and, again, made rounds. Every other night, we were on call for emergencies; we saw postoperative patients who had complications, assisted on emergency operations, visited patients in the emergency room, and worked up new patients who had been admitted for surgery.

My real education in surgery truly started during my early days at Mount

Sinai. There were some great surgeons there, and I got a close-up view of their handiwork on a daily basis; the best surgeons worked quickly and efficiently. The postoperative care of the patients was left to the residents, who called the surgeon's assistant when a complication developed.

But I learned more than just how to treat patients medically. I learned how arrogant surgeons could be. I witnessed political battles and the bitter competition, jealousy, and animosity that can exist among doctors. Most surgeons were gruff at the operating table. If they were dealing with a particularly troublesome operation, they were nasty to all the staff, especially the residents. (Regrettably, I later found that I, too, committed this same offense, often due to the stress of the moment.)

One day, I was scheduled to assist one of the busiest thoracic surgeons in town. He was removing the tubercular lung of a twenty-six-year-old woman, a common operation before the days of antituberculosis medications. He was a very capable surgeon, but he was particularly surly to residents. He never allowed us any responsibility, not even suturing. We just stood across from him at the operating table, occasionally sponging up blood and holding open the incision with retractors. Throughout the operation, the surgeon bragged about his wartime experiences. "I could have saved the leg of one German soldier," he said, "but I hated the Nazis, so I amputated it." Then he said, "You were probably in medical school during the war, Heimlich, and had your tuition paid for by the government." I didn't bother to correct the doctor; I simply could not have cared less for what he thought of me.

An hour after the operation ended, the nurse on the floor called me to come quickly to see the patient. I ran up to the ward and found that the patient was dead. On the floor was a large bottle to which the chest-drainage tube was attached. The bottle was filled with blood. The diagnosis was evident. When a lung is removed, a silk suture is tied around the large vein to the lungs before the blood vessel is cut so the lung can be removed. That suture had slipped, and the patient bled to death instantly. I called the surgeon and he rushed back to the ward. I stood with him as he faced the patient's parents. It was the first time I'd seen him appear humble.

When the end of my year's residency was approaching, it was time to apply for two additional years of training. I wanted to get those two years at

Mount Sinai Hospital because, as a second-year resident, I would have been allowed to perform all surgeries and had full responsibility for patients. That experience was required so that I could take both the American Board of Surgery and the American Board of Thoracic Surgery exams to become certified as a surgeon. Extending my residency at Mount Sinai was tough competition; only one person would be appointed, and there were lots of applicants. I believed I had a good chance for the position but lost out to another resident. I would have to find a residency at another hospital.

Even though I was armed with excellent recommendations from leading surgeons at Mount Sinai, the Jewish hospitals I applied to repeatedly turned me down. Thankfully, my father came to my rescue. Through his connections with the district attorney's office, Pop was able to get me a meeting with New York City's commissioner of health. When Pop and I sat down with him, the commissioner told us he had arranged for me to continue my residency at Bellevue Hospital. I would be guaranteed only one of the two years of residency that I required, but working at Bellevue was a plum I never could have attained on my own. Unlike private hospitals like Mount Sinai, Bellevue residents provided all the patient care, including surgery, under the supervision of staff surgeons.

The surgical experience at Bellevue turned out to be invaluable. In addition to carrying out the types of tasks I had done at Mount Sinai, I was also able to perform all kinds of surgery and in areas that were new to me, including abdominal surgery, orthopedics, and gynecology.

But the best part of being a surgical resident at Bellevue was coming upon a shocking discovery that would lead me to meeting the woman I would later marry.

8

SAVING A LIFE AND FINDING LOVE

Bellevue Hospital Center is run by the city of New York. It was founded in 1763, making it the oldest large-scale hospital in the United States. Bellevue pioneered the idea of the emergency room in 1869, when it was the first hospital to receive patients in horse-drawn ambulances. In the 1940s, when I began my medical career, I remember it was said that you could see all kinds of emergency situations at Bellevue, from car accident injuries to last-minute births.

What also made Bellevue unusual was that it contained various divisions, each overseen by a medical school, so the hospital offered residents like me unique learning opportunities. I was assigned to the Cornell Medical College division, and so all the patients in that division were under my care while I was on duty.

One night, I was making rounds in the emergency room, seeing my Cornell patients, when a nurse called me to pronounce a patient in another division dead. She summoned me because the patient's regular doctor was asleep and she did not want to wake him.

The man who lay before me had fallen out of a third-story window a few days before and had suffered multiple serious injuries. When I examined him, I saw that he was not breathing but I could find a weak pulse. Quickly, I observed his jaw, which was broken, and realized that his facial injuries were blocking his airway. I instantly performed a tracheotomy, inserting a tube through his neck and into his trachea to get air into his lungs. The man soon began breathing, a full pulse returned, and he regained consciousness.

The patient's name was Dick Yeatman. After saving his life, he was placed in my care. Over the next nine months, I treated his fractured jaw, broken legs, and other injuries, and I got to know him pretty well. Dick was in his forties and had nearly met his demise after he leaned out the window of his Fifth Avenue apartment to wipe it off and lost his balance. He was an officer of the Texaco Company and was married to a woman named Constance, or "Connie," as she was called. While Dick was being treated at Bellevue, Connie sat at his bedside every day. She was from a prominent Tennessee family, and often her friend Mary Dillon came along, too. Mary was a blue-eyed, soft-spoken Irish woman in her sixties, and she was also powerful. She was the first female chairperson of the board of a public utility company, the Brooklyn Union Gas Company, and had been appointed president of the New York Board of Education by Mayor Fiorello LaGuardia.

Dick and Connie loved opera and had box seats at the Metropolitan Opera House. One day, Connie asked if I would like to go in Dick's place. I accepted without hesitation, having been an opera fan since college. (At Cornell, I had taken a course on Wagner, and during the Christmas vacation of my junior year, I went with a friend to the Met to hear *Tannhäuser*, the first and only opera I'd ever attended.) Plus, the Yeatmans' seats were center parterre box seats, the best in the house. (They had originally been held by the industrialist Cornelius "Commodore" Vanderbilt.)

To get to the Met, I took a bus from Bellevue, dressed in my best suit. I thoroughly enjoyed the opera and was fortunate enough to join Connie, Mary, and several of their elderly women friends for other Saturday evening performances. As I took in the mesmerizing sounds of Verdi, Puccini, and Mozart, I considered myself the luckiest man on earth. But my luck was about to increase tenfold.

JANE

By Christmastime 1949, I was in my third year of residency. My year at Bellevue had drawn to a close, and Bellevue's chief of surgery, who also held that position at Triboro Hospital, helped me secure a position there as chief resident in surgery. Triboro Hospital was located in New York City and specialized in tuberculosis treatment. One day, Connie called me and said Mary Dillon was giving a dinner party for a young woman named Jane Murray, a writer who was visiting from San Francisco. Would I escort her? I agreed. To my surprise, Connie immediately put Jane on the phone, and we arranged that I would pick her up that night and take her to the party. It was a small dinner party with only a handful of couples. I remember the delicious steak dinner Mary served but little about Jane, except that she was very pretty. One guest spent the entire evening telling everyone about her recent honeymoon, so by the time Jane and I parted that evening, we still knew next to nothing about each other. The next day, Jane went back to San Francisco.

A year later, I again received a call from Connie Yeatman. "Guess who's visiting me?" she chirped. "It's that darling Jane Murray." Once again, Connie shoved the phone in Jane's hand. After some small talk, I asked what she was doing that night. She said she was fixing dinner for a sick friend. When I asked her what time she would be free, she told me ten o'clock. I said I would pick her up at her friend's house. (As it turned out, the sick "friend" was her boyfriend. I later learned he was not too happy about this arrangement.)

I picked up Jane and took her to a Howard Johnson's ice cream shop on the corner of Fifty-Ninth Street and Park Avenue. As we ate our ice cream, Jane asked me meaningful questions about my work, including my duty in China. She was a writer and I liked her inquisitive nature.

Jane wrote about that ice-cream date in her memoir *Out of Step*. As she described it, I chose "the least expensive option" for a place for us to get acquainted, noting that I was not getting paid a salary. Jane wrote that she quickly honed in on the fact that I wasn't a big talker, except where my work was concerned:

> Seated in a booth across from him, I studied his craggy good looks. The bushy eyebrows, a hawk-like nose, and firm chin complemented his lean six-foot frame. While he worked his way through two scoops of butter pecan ice cream, savoring each spoonful as if he wanted it to last forever, I plied him with questions. I knew he had been in China during the war.
>
> "What was China like?"
>
> "Interesting."
>
> He took another spoonful.

I plowed on. "Did you always want to be a doctor?"

"I guess so."

Years later, it came as no surprise when the man who became my husband admitted that he was uncomfortable talking one-on-one.

When I asked him about his work, I hit pay dirt. It turned out that his medical passion was the esophagus, which I soon learned was the tube that carries food from the throat to the stomach.

. . . I listened, entranced, to his medical talk.[1]

By the time we finished our ice cream, I looked across the table and thought, "I could marry this girl." (Years later, Jane let me know she had thought the same thing.) Soon after that, Jane decided to move back to New York and live with her parents.

I knew right off the bat that Jane and I came from two very different worlds. We were both Jewish, but that was about where the similarities ended. Whereas I had grown up in a family struggling to make ends meet, Jane had grown up in high society, the privileged daughter of celebrity parents. While Jane's grandparents on her father's side were Yiddish-speaking immigrants who were almost penniless when they settled in New York's Jewish Lower East Side, her father literally danced his way out of poverty. Arthur Murray (whose original name was Murray Teichman) had a mail-order dance-lesson business and built an empire of dance studios. Later, he and his wife, Kathryn, starred in the long-running, popular television show *The Arthur Murray Dance Party*. Jane had attended Shipley School (a boarding school in Pennsylvania) and Sarah Lawrence College.

At the end of our date at Howard Johnson's, I told her I would not be able to see her for a while because I was studying for the surgical board examinations. But then I called her the next morning and asked her out for dinner that night. When I arrived at the home of her parents, they were not there. Jane offered me a drink, and I asked for scotch and soda. It turned out Jane had never mixed a drink before and poured me a full glass of scotch with just a squirt of soda.

A little while later, her parents walked in. I was so tipsy, I could not stand up to greet them. Once I was able to get on my feet, the four of us had dinner at a lovely French restaurant nearby. Throughout the evening, I observed Jane's lovely way of addressing people and the sparkle of her eye, and I knew

I was hooked. For the next four months, we went out every evening. To hell with the surgery board exams.

After a month or two of dating, Kathryn and Arthur invited Jane and me to dinner at the Persian Room in the Plaza Hotel. Jane and I danced a few numbers, after which Kathryn asked me to dance. I was plenty nervous leading one of America's most famous women known for dancing, but I'm pleased to say I held my own. When Kathryn and I returned to the table, she said delightedly, "Arthur, Hank is a natural dancer."

Figure 8.1. *Son-in-law*: By marrying Jane, I inherited her energetic and fun-loving celebrity parents, Kathryn and Arthur Murray.

I turned to Arthur and said, "Arthur, you'd better treat me right, or I'll tell everyone I never took a lesson in my life."

But my father-in-law was just as quick. "Just don't tell them you took lessons at Arthur Murray's," he said in his usually wry manner.

A PROPOSAL OF MARRIAGE

That spring, I planned to ask Jane to marry me. She and I were to go skiing at a small resort in Massachusetts and stay at the home of my sister and her husband. In those days, a man and a woman going away together was unusual, but after a bit of convincing, Kathryn gave her approval. We had a wonderful time. When the moment hit me, we were making our way up the hill, each sitting on either side of a T-bar lift. The T-bar wasn't that steady, so I held off, afraid the shock might cause Jane to fall off.

Later that evening, as we were driving back to New York, I pulled off the highway so we could eat sandwiches Cele had packed for us. Within a few moments, I declared my love for Jane, and she told me she loved me, too.

"Since we love each other, we should get married," I said. And she agreed.

"Do you think September would be a good time?" I asked.

"That will be fine," she said.

I let out a big breath and started the car. As we continued driving down the parkway, I suddenly blurted, "Why wait? How about June?"

"That will be fine," she repeated.

After dropping Jane off at her house, I rushed home and woke my parents to tell them the happy news. They had gotten to know Jane when she had come to our home for dinner a few times. In fact, they had grown so fond of her that my mother said, "Henry, don't you ever hurt that wonderful girl. If you do, I will surely take her side."

Jane and I were married on June 3, 1951—exactly four months after our Howard Johnson's date—in a Jewish wedding ceremony at the Plaza Hotel. I later found out that Jane had never been crazy about being a celebrity's daughter, and she was content to have found a man who was "just a doctor." She noted in her memoir that she was delighted to shed my celebrity maiden name for one of an anonymous doctor. Surely, the name "Heimlich" was not likely to appear outside of a medical journal. I felt secure in knowing that I would at last be an ordinary person.

But the fates had something else in mind for me.[2]

In fact, I was about to devise my first significant medical innovation—one that would become known throughout the world.

Figure 8.2. *Wedding day*: Jane and I were married on June 3, 1951.

Figures 8.3 and 8.4. *Our early years together*: After Jane and I were married, we lived in New York City and then Rye, New York. Neither of us anticipated that I would make a big splash in the medical world so early in my career.

9

RESTORING THE ABILITY TO SWALLOW: THE REVERSED GASTRIC TUBE OPERATION

Soon after Jane and I were married, we moved in to an apartment in New York City on Madison Avenue near Fortieth Street. Jane then became pregnant with our son Philip, whom we named after my father. Philip was born in December of 1952, at a time when most obstetricians were giving patients anesthesia before they delivered. But when Jane went into labor and her doctor suggested he give her anesthesia, she fought him off. Even though it went contrary to medical trends of the day, Jane was interested in natural childbirth. (Decades later, she would make a name for herself in the field of holistic health by writing two books on the subject.)

Despite the many evenings I spent with Jane instead of studying for my exams, I had passed the tests. This qualified me as both a general and a thoracic surgeon. Now I had to find work and put to the test what I had learned in medical school, China, and my residency programs. Unfortunately, nothing I could find in the way of employment paid very much, so I had to take on as many jobs as I could. I was a staff surgeon at Mount Sinai Hospital. In addition, the chief of thoracic surgery at Montefiore Hospital had offered me a job as his assistant at both Montefiore and Mount Sinai Hospital, where he also practiced. He was a good chest surgeon and a pleasant, kind man. I assisted him in surgery and looked after his patients postoperatively; in return, he gave me a percentage of his fees for each operation, which altogether earned me $2,500 a year. I earned extra money treating employees of a department store and hotel association. Fortunately, I had a car, a Chevrolet sedan I used to zip around New York City from one job to the next. Parking was not often a problem; my license plate designated that I was a medical doctor, which allowed me to park almost anywhere.

At the same time, I rented space in a doctor's office in New York City, where I had begun a private practice. It was tricky trying to find patients. Unlike today, when surgeons of all ages can join an HMO or a partnership fairly quickly, building a practice in the early 1950s was like starting a business from scratch, and I would be competing for patients with older physicians with large practices. At that time, many patients had no insurance, and there was fierce competition among surgeons for patients who could pay. (Some surgeons engaged in fee splitting, where they would slip money, gifts, or other kickbacks to family practitioners who referred to them patients for surgery. One time, a physician referred a patient to me and expected some sort of payback. Being new, I did not understand the system and refused his request, after which he cursed me out and called me "tight." Throughout my career, I have always loathed the negativity that surrounds the business of medicine.)

TREATING PATIENTS WHO COULD NOT SWALLOW

Almost immediately after I began my practice, I took a special interest in patients who were unable to swallow due to a damaged esophagus, or swallowing tube. The condition of not being able to swallow or having difficulty swallowing is called *dysphagia*.

There are many ways that patients develop dysphagia. Some have an esophagus that is so inflamed, scarred, or ulcerated by chronic acid reflux from the stomach that their esophagus is blocked and useless. Other patients have cancer of the esophagus, and, in those cases, part or all of the esophagus must be removed. Some babies are born with an esophagus that is either closed off or connected to the trachea; in the latter case, any food or liquid swallowed enters into the airway, often causing death.

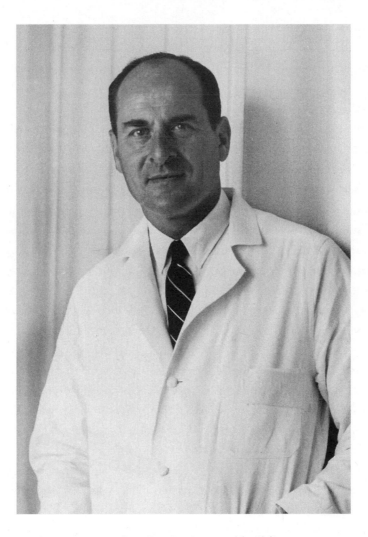

Figure 9.1. *My own practice*: Beginning and building my own practice took time and patience.

Back in the 1950s, when people were less aware of the dangers of caustic household cleaners, they would store lye under their sinks and keep the liquid, commonly used to open clogged drains, in glass soda-pop bottles. Children (and occasionally adults) often found the lye under the sink and, thinking the liquid inside was soda, drank it. Often this resulted in scarring or narrowing of the esophagus. Each year, thousands of children suffered with—or died from—a destroyed esophagus. Some adults intentionally drank lye to commit suicide. When those attempts failed, they were stricken with the inability to consume food.

In the cases where the esophagus has been severely damaged or destroyed, the outcome is the same: without a healthy esophagus, patients are denied the ability to swallow food and sometimes liquids. The life of a patient with dysphagia is extremely unpleasant. This was especially true back in the 1950s, when there was no adequate method to treat the condition. Since these individuals could not swallow saliva, they were condemned to a lifetime of drooling or constant spitting. To take in nourishment, patients had a tube with a funnel attached to it surgically inserted into the stomach. The funnel appeared outside the body. In order to "eat," patients first chewed food and then spat it into the funnel, where it would move into the stomach and be digested. Liquids were poured directly into the funnel. Sometimes the stomach tube, which was made of rubber or plastic, was damaged by the stomach's gastric acid and had to be replaced.

Being afflicted with dysphagia was a source of embarrassment for most patients. Some went to great lengths to hide their condition from friends, even family, for decades, conducting their feeding rituals at home, when they were alone, or in public-bathroom stalls. Many avoided socializing at events where food would be present.

Surgeons had been trying for years to devise an operation that would replace a defective esophagus. Researchers in this field were working largely on two methods. One consisted of first removing the part of the esophagus that was blocked or damaged and everything below it, ending at the junction where the esophagus meets the stomach. Then a hole was made at the top of the stomach of the same diameter as that of the esophagus. Finally, the dangling, remaining end of the esophagus was connected to the hole at the top of the stomach.

Using this technique allowed patients to eat; however, it did not solve a dangerous problem: stomach acid could rise up into the esophagus, which is a condition we call *acid reflux*. Most healthy people don't have to worry about acid reflux, because they have muscular tissue between the esophagus and stomach called the *gastroesophageal sphincter*. This sphincter acts as a valve to prevent acid from rising up into the esophagus and damaging it. But this first method surgeons were attempting, which pulled the stomach up to meet part of the esophagus, left the patient with no sphincter valve. As a result, acid reflux freely flowed upward and inflamed and ulcerated the esophagus, leading to bleeding ulcers and the scarring and closure of tissue. Sometimes, the ulcers bled and even perforated the stomach, allowing the organ to hemorrhage into the chest or abdomen, a condition that sometimes proved fatal.

The second method researchers were attempting proved just as harmful. Here, lengths of the patient's small or large intestine were used to replace the entire esophagus. As with the other procedure, this method left the patient without a sphincter valve, and so the rising stomach acid could cause the transplanted intestine to scar, close down, and bleed. In some cases, ulcers perforated the transplanted intestine, resulting in severe complications or death.

All in all, there was no effective surgical procedure that could restore these patients' ability to swallow. The only workable solution—however unpleasant—was the rubber feeding tube that had to be surgically inserted into the stomach. Seeing the agony that patients with dysphagia endured and the ineffective and dangerous treatments that were available in the 1950s made me determined to come up with a better way to replace someone's missing or deteriorated esophagus so that patients could enjoy a good quality of life.

CREATING A NEW ESOPHAGUS FROM THE STOMACH

In January 1950, I attended a thoracic surgical conference in San Francisco. Researchers gave presentations outlining the various methods, including the partial-esophagus-removal technique and the one that involved replacing the esophagus with part of the intestine, and the problems that stomach acid caused. However, one group of surgeons caught my attention; they reported that they had devised an approach that overcame the stomach-acid problem.

It had long been known that the upper third of the stomach, called the *cardia*, and the middle third of the stomach, or the *body*, both secrete acid. However, the lower third of the stomach, called the *antrum*, *neutralizes* acid, thereby preventing acid from entering the small intestine. Evolution explains why this is so: Our stomachs need the acid to digest food, but once the digested food is ready to leave the stomach and move into the small intestine, the acid must be gone. Otherwise, it would destroy the intestine. That is why the lowest part of the stomach shuts down acid secretion.

The researchers at the conference explained how they made use of this knowledge in experiments on dogs. First, the scientists removed the upper three-quarters of a dog's stomach, including the gastroesophageal sphincter. They then connected the remaining lower portion of the stomach—the part that does not secrete acid—to the lower end of the esophagus. For six months, the animals remained free of ulcers and other complications, even after they were injected with acid-stimulating drugs.

It was not an ideal solution, for the remaining stomach was quite small and the animals could eat food in only very small amounts. Also, each of the dogs that underwent these experiments still had a complete, healthy esophagus. Would the results be duplicated in patients whose esophagi were unhealthy or partially missing? It certainly did not offer a solution for patients who were missing their esophagus altogether.

But hearing about the dog experiments got me thinking: What if I replaced the esophagus using the lower portion of the stomach that neutral-izes acid? I thought about how I would leave the upper, acid-producing part of the stomach in place but make a tube from the lower part of the stomach. This tube would be the same diameter as that of the esophagus. One end of the tube would remain attached to the stomach, leaving the other end free. I would then lift the free end of the tube within the chest or through a tunnel under the skin and attach it to the remaining esophagus or the pharynx. Thus, the gastric tube would become the patient's new esophagus.

And here's the beautiful thing: the new esophagus could not be damaged by acid because it would have been made from the stomach, which tolerates acid. What's more, the upper portion of the esophagus would further resist acid because it was made from the acid-neutralizing antrum.

I thought of this method as a *reversed gastric tube operation.* "Reversed," because the tube created from the stomach would replace the esophagus by being brought upward, so it essentially functions in reverse.

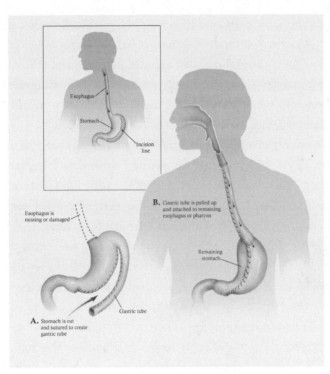

Figure 9.2. *Reversed gastric tube operation*: To treat a patient with severe swallowing problems, a tube is created from the stomach and brought up to replace part or all of the esophagus. (Illustration © Christy Krames 2013.)

As I visualized the method of making use of the stomach's lower region, I began to see that it could offer numerous advantages: First, the tube created from the stomach would come from the antrum, the lower, nonacidic part. This would eliminate the chances of stomach acid damaging the newly created "esophagus." Second, the lower part of the stomach offers more organ to work with, allowing for a sufficiently long, new esophagus. Third, three-quarters of the stomach would remain in the abdomen, so the stomach could function quite normally.

The fourth advantage concerns blood supply. I knew the blood supply to the newly created esophagus had to accompany it into the chest. Otherwise, the organ would die. Blood supply is also a critical component of replacing organs in children, for without a blood supply, the organ cannot grow as the child ages. A normal stomach has two blood supplies—one that supplies blood to the right side, and one that supplies blood to the left. The left side is the place from which the gastric tube would be cut. Creating the tube from the left side would ensure that the new organ maintains its own blood supply while the right side's blood supply would not be disturbed.

There was a fifth benefit—one I could not have fully realized at the time. Back in the 1950s, surgeons had not yet begun to replace human organs in patients using either transplanted organs from other individuals or artificially made ones. There was no artificial heart, for example. What we learned as we began doing organ replacement was that the body often rejects the new organs, and they stop working. Because my reversed gastric tube method was designed to use the patient's *own* organs, there was little chance of rejection.

I set about carefully analyzing my procedure to determine if it could work. I had many questions: Would the length of the gastric tube be adequate? Would its blood supply be sufficient? Would the parts be sufficiently mobile to extend to the neck? After studying the size of the organs involved and how they behaved, I determined that the procedure had strong potential and wanted to try it out on animals. But what medical college would allow a thirty-three-year-old doctor who had done no known scientific work to date to conduct research in its laboratories? My only solid contacts were at Montefiore Hospital, but it had no research laboratory or college. Mount Sinai Hospital started an animal-research laboratory in 1953, but when I inquired, I was turned down because the head of surgery was interested only in heart-surgery experiments.

Then I thought about New York Medical College and decided to pay the director of surgery a visit. It was impulsive. I did not know his name, nor did I try to make an appointment. I simply walked into the hospital and asked if I could speak to the director of surgery at the information desk. The woman there said his name was Dr. James Winfield and told me where his office was. When I got to his office, I explained to the secretary that I was a surgeon with a promising new idea, and I asked if I could see Dr. Winfield. Amazingly, he agreed to see me on the spot.

Dr. Winfield was a friendly man who listened attentively as I described the reversed gastric tube operation's concept. He asked some pertinent questions and said he would consider it. A few weeks later, he called me: "We can make you a clinical assistant professor in surgery so you can conduct this research. There's no pay, but you'll have access to the animal lab and a three-hundred-dollar grant."

I could hardly contain my excitement. This was the chance I had been looking for. Now I had access to a lab where I could truly test my idea to see if it did in fact allow people with dysphagia to be able to swallow.

SUCCESS IN THE LABORATORY

In 1954, I began a series of experiments to test the efficacy of the reversed gastric tube operation with dogs. With such a limited budget, I couldn't afford to hire any assistants, so I did all the work myself. The first attempt took eight or nine hours, and, sadly, the dog died. I experimented on a second dog, and it died, too. I didn't believe that their deaths were caused by a problem with the technique but rather the prolonged surgery and technical difficulties due to the fact that I was taking on too much myself. I obviously needed help. Things began to look up after I piqued the interest of a bright, young Mount Sinai resident who volunteered to help me on his days off. With his assistance, the subsequent procedures went faster and easier, and, thereafter, the dogs lived.

After a couple of days, I felt that a dog who had undergone the procedure might be ready to try drinking. I gave the dog some milk, and he drank it. I was hopeful. A few days later, I tried small amounts of meat, and the dog was able to eat. I knew then that the reversed gastric tube operation had strong potential to overcome dysphagia. But there was still one more test to do. Three weeks after the operation, I inserted barium into the dog's throat to trace its swallowing activity, and an x-ray showed the reversed gastric tube was functioning as a normal esophagus.

Figure 9.3. *In the laboratory*: I spent many hours in the laboratory, perfecting what would come to be known as the reversed gastric tube operation.

After I successfully completed the procedure on six dogs, I authored a paper along with Dr. Winfield, describing the results. "The Use of a Gastric Tube to Replace or By-Pass the Esophagus," published in *Surgery* in 1955,[1] was my first scientific paper. I knew that it was time to try out the reversed gastric tube operation on a human patient. It took a while before we had the right candidate. One day, a sixty-four-year-old patient with a metastasized cancer of the esophagus was admitted to Metropolitan Hospital, one of the three hospitals affiliated with New York Medical College. His esophagus was blocked by cancer, and he could no longer swallow food. I requested permission to perform the procedure. The hospital, chief of surgery, and patient all gave their consent. In August 1957, I replaced the cancerous part of the man's esophagus using my reversed gastric tube method. The procedure went beautifully, and, within two weeks, the patient was eating solid food. The man reported in April of 1958 that he was comfortable and able to eat without difficulty.

I was eager to tell my colleagues about this new procedure that had given the patient a newfound ability to eat. I presented the patient's case at the weekly surgical meeting in front of some thirty surgeons at New York Medical College. I felt sure the other surgeons would be ecstatic about my discovery.

After I described the operation, the patient was brought to the conference room. I had already arranged for an orderly to bring in a sandwich and a cup of coffee, which now sat in front of the patient. After describing his history, physical findings, and the reversed gastric tube operation, I said to him, "Please, go ahead and take a bite of your sandwich."

The patient eyed the sandwich before him.

"I can't eat," he said. Much to my chagrin, I heard roars of laughter among the surgeons. I waited for the laughter to subside.

"Sir, I saw you eat yesterday. Why can't you eat?"

"Because they didn't bring my teeth up from my room!" he bellowed. I smiled and asked the orderly to fetch the man's dentures. The room was silent.

We all waited until the orderly returned with the dentures and gave them to the patient. He then put them in his mouth, picked up the sandwich, took a big bite, and methodically chewed. When he was ready, the patient swallowed, and the bite of sandwich went down easily. The man smiled grandly and took another bite. Another swallow. Another smile. I myself was all grins, too. But, as the patient finished the sandwich, I couldn't help noticing that the doctors at the meeting just sat there glumly, none of them uttering a word.

I was ecstatic that I had proven that the reversed gastric tube operation could restore a patient's ability to eat. But, at the same time, I was disheartened that none of the surgeons seemed to appreciate my achievement. Still, I grew to expect this kind of rejection. In fact, when the reversed gastric tube procedure first became known, physicians seemed loathe to endorsing it or even acknowledging its benefits. Chiefs of surgery seemed to resent my work. At national surgical meetings, prominent surgeons bitterly spoke out against the procedure. (Many years later, I realized that, in the case of the reversed gastric tube operation, I had committed a medical faux pas, for I had not included my chiefs of surgery as authors of most of my papers. The practice of tying others to one's work, known as "academic slavery," was customary, even though the secondary physicians had not actually contributed to the work. I had committed a cardinal sin in the medical profession by not including their names.)

PATIENTS BENEFIT FROM THE REVERSED GASTRIC TUBE OPERATION

Soon, more and more physicians were finding out about the procedure—some surgeons were performing it—and other doctors referred to me patients who needed it. I remember the case of one patient in particular. Fifty-two-year-old Virginia Dixon had been in her early twenties when she had accidentally swallowed lye, leaving her esophagus scarred and blocked. Several attempts had been made to open the damaged part of her esophagus, but none had worked. For those twenty-nine years of not being able to swallow, Ms. Dixon fed herself in a way that most of us would think would severely cramp her quality of life. At each meal, she attached a funnel to a large, rubber feeding tube that had been surgically inserted into her stomach. Then she would chew her food, remove it from her mouth, and put it into the funnel so it could find a way to her stomach. Understandably, eating was a source of stress for Ms. Dixon, both emotionally and physically, for if food reached the back of her throat, she would choke and gag. Saliva pooled in the back of her throat, so she had to spit frequently.

Remarkably, Ms. Dixon hid her disability from her coworkers for decades by taking her tube feedings in a stall in the ladies' room at the office where she worked. Like many victims who are unable to swallow, her abnormal eating practices made it impossible for her to enjoy meals with family and friends. Yet Mrs. Dixon was a courageous, happy person who was married with two children. I felt humbled and privileged each time I spoke to this impressive woman.

In 1959, Ms. Dixon entered Montefiore Hospital and I performed the reversed gastric tube operation on her. Two weeks later, I brought Ms. Dixon a dish of gelatin. The gelatin product's flavor and texture helped patients who had not swallowed in a long time get the food down their throats without gagging or aspirating. The hospital photographer was present as Ms. Dixon raised the spoon to her lips, capturing in three pictures her experience of swallowing for the first time in twenty-nine years: In the first photograph, she is inserting a spoonful of gelatin into her mouth and appears dubious. In the second photo, she looks grim as she hesitates before actually swallowing. In the third photo, she has a joyful, broad smile and her eyes are gleaming as the gelatin goes down. The series of shots was published around the world.

Figure 9.4. *The swallow heard 'round the world:* Virginia Dixon was one of the first patients to undergo the reversed gastric tube operation. The media widely covered her first time eating in nearly thirty years.

Cosmopolitan magazine picked up the story. Protecting Ms. Dixon's identity, the article used the fictitious name, "Mrs. Dennis." The article was titled "Mrs. Dennis and the Miraculous Meal" and was written by esteemed medical writer Lawrence Galton. Mr. Galton described the process of the operation, which was followed by artificial-tube feedings while the body healed. "Then came the longed-for time—the first day of swallowing," Mr. Galton wrote:

Tentatively, she put it [the gelatin] in her mouth and tasted it, then looked at the nurse and doctor. Finally, she swallowed it—and gasped with delight. It was the first time in twenty-nine years that she had had the simple satisfaction of swallowing food.

An ingenious operation had made it possible—an operation which gave her a new esophagus, that tube which connects the pharynx with the stomach. And, that operation now promises to make possible normal lives for many cancer victims and for those who are injured from swallowing lye.[2]

Word continued to spread about what the media was calling the "Heimlich Reversed Gastric Tube operation." By this time, the procedure did not take as long as when I first performed it, thanks to a device developed by a Japanese physician specifically for the reversed gastric tube operation after he heard me give a lecture on it in Japan in 1958. The Izukura stapling instrument sped up the procedure by inserting two rows of staples that closed the incisions made to the stomach.

On July 7, 1961, an article appeared in *Life* magazine, whose caption called the procedure a "Hot Medical Discovery."[3] It shows a picture of me demonstrating the operation at an exhibit during a conference of the American Medical Association. At the exhibit, a patient who had undergone the procedure sat nearby, and I stood in our booth, talking to the doctors who approached. My dear friends Bernie and Ronnie Birnbaum had helped put it all together. Bernie, a producer at CBS, had assisted me in designing the exhibit, and Ronnie, who was a puppeteer, had constructed to my specifications a cloth model of a stomach, complete with zippers that showed how each step of the procedure is done. (Years later, my twin daughters, Janet and Elisabeth, would play with the model when they were young, although they had no idea what it represented.)

My good friend Paul Winchell, the famous ventriloquist, was also there. Paul had always loved medicine. Before he became an entertainer, he helped me educate other doctors about my reversed gastric tube operation. Paul frequently made rounds with me and made interesting suggestions in regard to patient care.

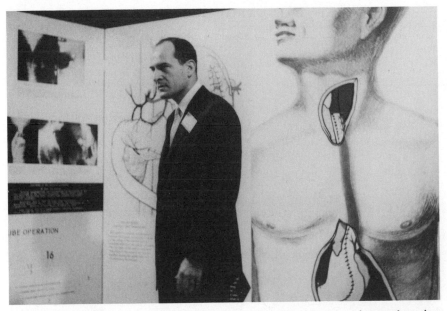

Figure 9.5. *Telling the world about the Heimlich reversed gastric tube operation*: I was eager to talk about this procedure that could restore patients' ability to swallow.

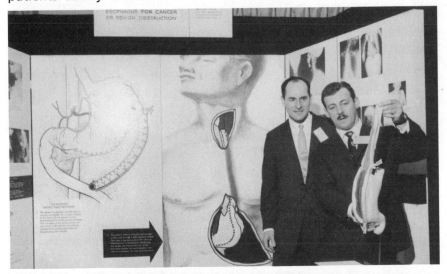

Figure 9.6. *An eager assistant*: Before he became a famous ventriloquist, Paul Winchell, who loved medicine, helped me educate other doctors about my reversed gastric tube operation.

AN INFANT UNDERGOES THE PROCEDURE

But even as the reversed gastric tube operation achieved great success, there was still a group of important candidates for the operation who had not yet benefited from it: children. There are different ways that children become inflicted with dysphagia. For example, some drink a caustic substance that burns and scars the esophagus. Some infants are born with a birth defect known as a tracheoesophageal fistula, in which the esophagus is attached to the trachea, thereby preventing the patients from being able to swallow food or liquids. To make matters worse, this condition causes them to inhale saliva into their lungs, causing pneumonia. One such infant was Guy Carpico.

Guy was born at Syosset Hospital in Long Island, New York, on December 24, 1965. Due to his tracheoesophageal fistula, Guy's esophagus was sealed off. Not only was Guy unable to swallow, he also had trouble breathing. Because his esophagus and trachea were connected, saliva would enter Guy's lungs, leaving him in danger of drowning in his own fluids. Guy's mother was referred by a physician who knew how I had helped other patients with severe swallowing problems. And so Guy was brought to Montefiore Hospital and put under my care when he was three days old.

Restoring Guy's ability to swallow was extremely complicated, much more so than other reversed gastric tube operations I had performed. Not only was I dealing with a very small body, but he also required seven operations both to correct the esophageal blockage and just to keep him alive. During his stay, the hospital staff had grown fond of Guy—one nurse refused to take a vacation until he was out of danger. I grew close to the infant, too. Concerned about his wellbeing, I sometimes slept in his hospital room. After nine months of treatment, Guy was finally able to breathe and eat normally.[4]

From the time he left the hospital before his first birthday to now, Guy and I have stayed in touch. When he was six years old, he visited my family in Cincinnati. (He still remembers playing with my twin daughters.) Today, Guy is a paramedic and emergency-medical-services instructor. He has told me that he went into the medical field after he understood how I had helped him as a surgeon and was dedicated to doing all I could to ensure his survival.

Figure 9.7. *A young patient*: In 1966, nine-month-old Guy Carpico has a new esophagus so he can swallow food and liquids. (From staff photographer/*New York Daily News*.)

By the early 1970s, I had performed the reversed gastric tube operation on more than fifty patients and had published in medical journals more than twenty-five scientific papers on the reversed gastric tube operation.[5] The operation became the standard procedure for dysphagia and was performed by surgeons around the world.

Prior to my development of the reversed gastric tube operation, researchers had been experimenting for more than fifty years, trying to help patients with a blocked or destroyed esophagus to be able to swallow food. What led to patients being able to perform the simple act of eating a sandwich was the fact that I had zeroed in on the problems that had limited these early pioneers and then figured out a way to overcome those obstacles.

Yet, back when I began performing the procedure, I learned an astonishing fact: I was not the first surgeon to do it. In October of 1955, I received a letter from a physician in a country that had been cut off from the rest of the world, informing me of this fact. That discovery led to an incredible journey to Eastern Europe.

10

PERFORMING THE REVERSED GASTRIC TUBE OPERATION BEHIND THE IRON CURTAIN

hile I was working on developing the reversed gastric tube operation, it never occurred to me that another surgeon had come up with the same procedure. But in October 1955, I received a letter from Dr. Dan Gavriliu from Bucharest, Romania. He said that he had read in a medical journal about my reversed gastric tube procedure and wanted to inform me that he had been performing it since 1951.

Considering where Dr. Gavriliu lived, it's no wonder that I had not heard about his work. During the Cold War between the United States and the Soviet Union, Romania had been isolated behind the Iron Curtain. Most publications from outside the country never reached the USSR, but certain international publications were allowed in. Dr. Gavriliu had read an abstract of the 1955 *Surgery* article in *International Abstracts of Surgery*.[1]

Dr. Gavriliu and I began exchanging letters. He explained that he had first performed the procedure on April 20, 1951, four years before I had done so. Writing in perfect English, he invited me to Romania as a guest of government-controlled Society of Medical Science. He said he wanted us to get together to compare our experiences and even operate alongside each other. Because our two countries had no diplomatic relations, there was no Romanian embassy in Washington; however, there was, he informed me, a Romanian legation, and a travel visa awaited me should I decide to accept his offer.

115

4   Standard-Star, New Rochelle, N. Y.—Sat., Sept. 15, 1956

CHANCE PERUSAL by a Romanian physician of a medical journal containing an article by a Rye surgeon, led to an invitation to Dr. and Mrs. Henry Heimlich of 851 Forest Avenue, Rye, to visit Romania. They will leave Monday. The article dealt with a new technique employed in certain types of esophagus operations. It was devised and performed successfully by Dr. Heimlich, who has offices at 140 Lockwood Avenue, New Rochelle, and is on the staff of New Rochelle Hospital. The Heimlichs also will go to Russia where Dr. Heimlich hopes to meet Soviet surgeons. Mrs. Heimlich is the former Jane Murray, daughter of Mr. and Mrs. Arthur Murray, noted dance masters. The Heimlichs are pictured with special camera with which he hopes to film foreign operating procedures. They have two young sons—Staff Photo by John Marrone

New Rochelle Surgeon
To Visit Iron Curtain Land

A chance perusal by a Rumanian physician of a medical journal containing an article by a Rye surgeon, led to an invitation to Dr. and Mrs. Henry Heilich, 851 Forest Avenue, to visit Rumania. They will leave Monday, with Paris as the first stop.

The article, dealing with a new technique employed in certain types of esophagus operations, was devised and successfully performed by Dr. Heimlich, who maintains offices at 140 Lockwood Avenue, New Rochelle, and who is a member of the staff of New Rochelle Hospital.

After reading the article, Dr. Dan Gavriliu of the Rumanian Society of Medical Science wrote Dr. Heimlich in praise of the work.

After three months of correspondence, the invitation to visit his country came at the request of the Rumanian Academy of Science in order that the two surgeons might exchange data on the techniques of chest operations.

After visiting Paris, the Heimlichs will head for Bucharest, via Berlin, and later will go to Russia for nearly two weeks in Kiev, Leningrad and Moscow, where Dr. Heimlich hopes to have the opportunity to meet other surgeons. After visits to Copenhagen, Amsterdam and Brussels, the couple will head for home, arriving in New York Oct. 21.

Dr. Heimlich is a graduate of New Rochelle High School, Cornell University and its Medical Schol and completed a residency in general surgery and in chest surgery in New York, before opening offices at his present location. He is the son of Mr. and Mrs. Philip Heimlich, of New York, formerly of New Rochelle.

During the war Dr. Heimlich served with Naval Group China (SACO), spending two years in a Japanese-held area of Inner Mongolia. He was one of a group of a dozen men responsible for gathering intelligence information and for radioing weather reports to the American Fleet in the Pacific. The group was also in charge of a 800-man guerrilla army. With his medical background, Dr. Heimlich who served as a lieutenant (S.G.) cared for the area war lord, his family and staff.

Among the gifts given the physician by the war lord in appreciation of his services was a banner which adorns a wall in the Heimlich home. It reads: "To Lieut. Dr. H. J. Heimlich—the people of Shenga, Suiyuan, thank him for giving us health and life."

Mrs. Heimlich is the former Jane Murray, daughter of Mr and Mrs Arthur Murray, noted dance masters. The Heimlichs have two sons, Philip, three-and-a-half, and Peter, two-and-a-half.

Figure 10.1. *Getting ready for an unusual trip*: Jane and I were excited about the prospect of being permitted a rare glimpse behind the Iron Curtain. (From "New Rochelle Surgeon to Visit Iron Curtain Land," *Standard-Star* [New Rochelle, NY], Saturday, September 15, 1956.)

What an opportunity, I thought. I had become so used to American doctors refusing to acknowledge the success of the reversed gastric tube procedure. Also, I was not aware of any other American scientist or doctor who had been permitted to enter Romania.

At the time I received Dr. Gavriliu's letter, Romania—or the Romanian People's Republic, as it was then called—was a Communist, Soviet-aligned, Eastern Bloc state. When World War II ended, Romania's economy was in decline, partly due to its having to pay war reparations to the Soviet Union. In the 1950s, however, Romania's Communist government began to assert more independence and induced the withdrawal of all Soviet troops by 1958. During this period, many people were executed or died in custody. While judicial executions between 1945 and 1964 numbered 137, deaths in custody are estimated in the tens of hundreds of thousands. Many more were imprisoned for political, economic, or other reasons and suffered abuse, torture, and, very often, death.

In early spring of 1956, I accepted Dr. Gavriliu's invitation, making two requests: I wanted to bring Jane, and I also wanted the operation filmed. Both requests were granted.

"I hope your honoured wife and yourself will enjoy the voyage," Dr. Gavriliu wrote in a letter dated July 17, 1956.

OFF TO ROMANIA

Getting to Romania involved a circuitous series of flights. We first flew from New York to West Berlin, then we crossed the border into Communist East Berlin by walking through the famous Brandenburg Gate next to the Berlin Wall. After a brief hassle with the Communist bureaucrats, they stamped our passports with East German visas. We then caught a flight on the government-controlled Air Romine and boarded a twelve-person, twin-engine propeller plane to Bucharest.

2   The Daily Item, Port Chester, N. Y., Tues., Sept. 25, 19
RYE-HARRISON

DR. HENRY HEIMLICH of 851 Forest Avenue, Rye, noted chest surgeon, is shown with Mrs. Heimlich at International Airport prior to their departure to Brussels, via Sabena Belgian World Airlines. Dr. Heimlich who has his offices at 140 Lockwood Avenue, New Rochelle, has been invited by the Society of Medical Science to exchange data on the technique of chest operations. Mrs. Heimlich is the former Jane Murray, daughter of Mr. and Mrs. Arthur Murray.

Figure 10.2. *Ready for takeoff*: A number of newspapers covered our trip because it was highly unusual for outsiders to be allowed into Romania. (From the *Daily Item* [Port Chester, NY], Tuesday, September 25, 1956.)

On arrival at the Bucharest airport, we were greeted by a group of officials and physicians, including Dr. Gavriliu. He was a thin, good-looking man about my age, thirty-six. Young girls dressed in Romanian peasant costumes presented flowers to Jane. To us, two Americans who had little idea of what goes on in authoritarian regimes, it seemed as if we were going to have a pleasant, relaxing time. We checked in at the Athénée Palace, a comfortable, old hotel on a square.

The next morning, a government car picked me up and took me to the university hospital to perform the reversed gastric tube operation. Dr. Gavriliu was inside the car. The hospital was large and quite modern. I later found out it had been a Catholic hospital originally and then had been taken over by the government. We went directly to an operating room where a patient who had cancer of the esophagus was already anesthetized.

Dr. Gavriliu and I scrubbed our hands and forearms, and a nurse held a sterile rubber glove for me to slip into. As I slid my hand into it, the glove ripped apart. The same thing happened with the second and third gloves I attempted to put on. I was to learn that in poverty-stricken Romania, the medical staff did not have the luxury of using gloves once and then discarding them, as we did in the United States. These gloves had been used, sterilized, and reused again and again. On the next attempt to don the gloves, I gingerly slipped my hands into them, and they remained intact.

Gavriliu and I performed the operation together, which took the whole day. Toward the last few hours, a strange thing happened. The assistants, one by one, walked away from the operating table, leaving Gavriliu and me to finish the operation on our own. I assumed the reason was that the Communists considered all workers equal; meaning that, unlike in the United States, operating-room assistants were not responsible to any surgeon's authority. I sensed that Gavriliu was angry, having to complete so much of the work himself, although he could do nothing about it.

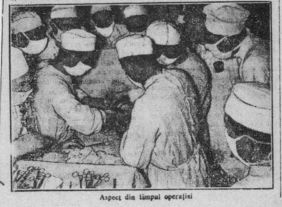

Figure 10.3. *Making headlines behind the Iron Curtain*: My collaborating with Dr. Dan Gavriliu in the operating room was covered by the Romanian press. (From "Demonstratie de esofagoplastie dupa procedeul dr. Dan Gavriliu," *Muncitorul Sanitar* [Romania], September 29, 1956.)

SECRECY AND A COMMUNIST GOVERNMENT

After the operation, we walked back to the hotel and Dr. Gavriliu stopped me on the street, offering me a quiet caution.

"Do not talk about anything in your hotel room," he said. "The walls are bugged." I nodded, both surprised and concerned. I never imagined that I would be the focus of Cold War spying, but it actually made sense. I was one of a very few American doctors—if not the only American doctor—to visit Romania since the start of the Cold War. I began to wonder if the trip had been Dr. Gavriliu's idea or the government's.

Jane and I were in Bucharest for one week. As the days progressed, I would hear other people whisper similar warnings to us as we walked outside, away from any hidden microphones. At every function we attended, we noticed a mean-looking guy, always smoking, whose title was "Secretary of the Medical Society." We later learned that he was really a member of the Bucharest secret police sent to keep an eye on us.

A fine, young medical student was assigned to guide us around Bucharest. When we were walking outside and not within earshot of anyone else, he told us about some of his professors who had been taken away by the secret police and never heard from again. Others were sent to work on the construction of the Moscow Canal only to show up again, years later, emotionally and physically destroyed.

The next day, the medical student did not show up as he had done on other mornings. We asked our handlers that day where he was, and they told us he was visiting his grandmother. We quietly continued our investigation, asking people we felt we could trust where the young man might be and learned that the visiting-the-grandmother line actually meant someone had been picked up by government authorities. Alarmed, we got in touch with the chargé d'affaires of the American legation; unfortunately, he explained, he was not allowed contact with Romanian officials. Instead, he could only advise us.

"Keep asking for the young man," the chargé d'affaires said. "Tell your contacts that you'd like to see him." We kept asking, and it worked. The next day, the student was back with us, to our great relief.

One day, while Jane and I were out walking with Dr. Gavriliu, we learned the truth about how our trip came to be. "I did not want you to come to Romania," I remember Dr. Gavriliu confiding. "The government told me to invite you because they saw us working together as a way to improve our relationship with the United States. They ordered me to send the letter inviting you here. After that, they suspected me of treason because I had made contact with you. Now I am under house arrest." Later, I suspected that it had not been Dr. Gavriliu who had spotted the abstract about the reversed gastric tube operation in the international medical journal but Romanian government officials.

A few days before Jane and I were to leave, Dr. Gavriliu told me that the Romanian Medical Society would be hosting a reception and dinner in my honor. "Is there anyone you would like to invite?" he asked. I immediately answered that I would like to invite the American chargé d'affaires and his staff, since they had expressed a desire to improve relations with Romania. On our last night, the Americans came to the party and, for the first time, had unofficial contact with Romanians. Subsequently, because of that contact, the American representatives were temporarily allowed to arrange showings of American surgical films to the Romanian doctors once a month.

~~~

After we returned back home, Dr. Gavriliu and I kept in contact. He sent me letters updating me on the conditions of patients he and I had operated on. I assumed that his letters were being censored by the authorities, yet I still appreciated what appeared to be genuine appreciation for our relationship.

"When we parted at the aerodrome, I felt a couple of friends [were] leaving us. The thoughts and best wishes of people you knew here accompanied both of you all over your travel," he wrote in a letter dated November 22, 1956. In asking about whether Jane enjoyed the trip back, Dr. Gavriliu wrote, "It was a pity we did not have the opportunity to dance and let me learn the new [dances]. I love dancing [to] good music."

Given that Jane and I had been offered the rare opportunity to peak behind the Iron Curtain, our arrival back in the United States generated quite a lot of media interest. When interviewed by the press, I complimented the surgeons and students of Eastern Europe, but I also minced no words in complaining about the conditions under which they had to work and the inability of the people to benefit from medical successes.

"It is remarkable what outstanding work is being done by individual practitioners in Romania under very poor conditions," I told the *Westchester News*. "Their operating rooms are very poor, and although the interiors are clean, the hospitals are very old. They are far behind us in the general status of medical care."[2]

On December 11, 1956, I gave a talk to a medical organization in Paramus, New Jersey, where I showed movies and slides of the procedures I had performed with Dr. Gavriliu and other medical staff. I explained how the surgeons worked all day and halfway through the night and with inferior equipment, all while being hounded by the government.

"They were beat, but they did this remarkable work," I said.[3]

Despite my harsh words, I was invited back to Romania in 1960 to again perform the reversed gastric tube operation with Dr. Gavriliu. By this time, I had published a January 18, 1957, article in *Surgery* titled "The Use of a Gastric Tube to Replace the Esophagus as Performed by Dr. Dan Gavriliu of Bucharest, Romania."[4] I had also authored a paper that appeared in the medical journal *Diseases of the Chest* in 1959. In that article, I described how Dr. Gavriliu got in touch with me in 1955 and let me know how he had been performing the reversed gastric tube operation since 1951, how he and I performed the procedure together in Romania in 1956 (which was recorded on film), and how Dr. Gavriliu and I reported the results of the operation at the Meeting of the International Society of Surgery in 1957.[5] (In addition, I published numerous other scientific articles between 1959 and 1971 in which I also credited the physician's work.)

On the second trip to Romania, the operation was again captured on film. Upon my return to the United States, Baxter Laboratories, then the principal manufacturer of intravenous solutions, provided funds for me to edit and distribute a movie, which carried the not-so-glamorous title, "Esophageal Replacement with a Reversed Gastric Tube." In 1961, Baxter submitted it to the Fourth International Film Festival of Medical-Scientific Films in Turin, Italy, where it was awarded a Bronze Medallion of Minerva.[6]

Figure 10.4. *A critical voice*: When Jane and I returned from Romania, I complained to the American media about healthcare conditions in Eastern Europe. (From Mary Tanenbaum, "County Surgeon Finds Reds Ailing," *Westchester (NY) News*, Thursday, January 31, 1957.)

Dr. Dan Gavriliu died in 2012 at the age of 97. Without question, he deserves credit for being the first surgeon to discover and perform the procedure that would become known as the Heimlich-Gavriliu Reversed Gastric Tube operation. It was the first successful replacement of a human organ. I am honored to consider myself a colleague of Dr. Gavriliu's, one of the world's great pioneers in thoracic surgery.

Still, I am proud of the fact that I was the first surgeon in the Western world to perform the reversed gastric tube operation. And I am heartened that it became the medical standard to treat dysphagia and is used by surgeons throughout the world.

11

A PROMISE TO A DEAD SOLDIER KEPT: THE HEIMLICH CHEST DRAIN VALVE

It had been twenty years since the Chinese soldier in Inner Mongolia had died on my makeshift operating table after receiving a bullet wound to the chest. And yet the memory still haunted me. I could remember seeing his chest filled with blood and air, which pressed on his lung, causing it to collapse. Without the ability to expand, the lung could not take in air.

I continued to ask myself what I could have done to save him. Was it possible that there existed a simple, logical solution to keeping the lung expanded?

The problem of a lung collapsing is not only life threatening for victims of bullet wounds. I have seen it time and again among patients who have undergone chest surgery, such as when a surgeon operates on the esophagus, lung, or heart, or even when a doctor merely inserts a needle into the chest to obtain a lung biopsy. The condition of a lung collapsing is known as *pneumothorax*. If not treated immediately, the person can no longer breathe, and death quickly follows. In 1962, I wrote about this dilemma in a book called *Postoperative Care in Thoracic Surgery*.

A major reason why a lung collapses is because there is pressure on it due to surrounding fluid or air or both. Therefore, it's essential to remove the air and fluid to allow the lung to expand. In the early 1960s, doctors had a rather primitive way to do this. First, they drained the buildup of air and fluid by inserting a tube into the chest and connecting it to a suction machine attached to the wall or floor of the patient's room. A series of two or three bottles, which usually sat on the floor, collected the buildup.

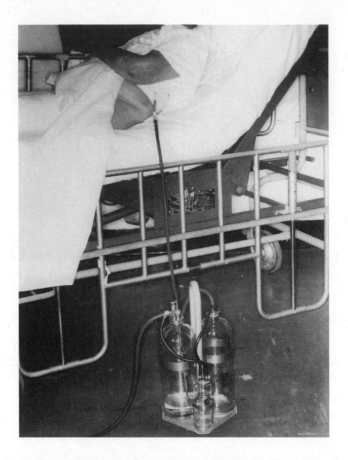

Figure 11.1. *The old way*: Before the Heimlich Chest Drain Valve, patients who had undergone chest surgery were hooked up to cumbersome suction devices and collection bottles.

This method was awkward and potentially dangerous. It greatly limited the patient's movement and proved cumbersome for hospital staff who had to move the patient to another room. Also, there was the chance that the tube draining fluid from the chest could be accidentally yanked out. The situation for soldiers in the field who had received a chest wound was even more precarious. Setting up the ungainly chest-drainage system was simply not feasible, and so, sadly, many soldiers died when shot on the battlefield.

THE ANSWER: A VALVE

I began to investigate what it would take to design a new chest-drainage mechanism that would allow air and fluid to leave the chest so that the lung could expand and let the patient breathe. But this mechanism would have to do something else that was critical: it had to prevent the air and fluid from returning to the chest. If it did get back in, the lung would again collapse. That was what the suction caused by the bottle setup accomplished.

But was suction necessary? I didn't think so because the air and fluid would naturally leave the body as the lung expanded. The most important thing was to *not allow the air and fluid to get back into the chest*.

And that's when it hit me: Why not just use a valve, one that permitted the air and fluid to drain away from the chest and not return? If the right valve was in place, there would be no backup to worry about, and the lung could function normally.

But which valve was the right one? I began to think about all the different kinds of valves that were out there. There was a ball valve in which a metal ball lies on top of the opening of a tube. As fluid or air comes up through the tube, it pushes the ball out of place. When the flow stops, the ball falls right back into place, thereby preventing fluid and air from backing up.

But a ball valve wouldn't work. If the valve's opening turned sideways or upside down, the ball would not fall into position to shut off the valve.

What about a flap valve, such as the kind you see in toilets? A flap valve opens and closes on a hinge, cutting off the flow of liquids and air when they reach a certain level. But that, too, posed a problem because, if a blood clot lodged under the lid of the valve, it would stay open, allowing air and fluid to flow back into the chest.

I knew of only one other type of valve, a flutter valve. This is a piece of soft tubing, usually made of rubber or soft plastic. When air or fluid enters one end of the tube, it opens, allowing the air or fluid to pass through. After that, the tube flattens again.

Here's how I envisioned the flutter valve working to drain air and fluid from a patient's chest: As the patient inhales, there would be pressure in the chest as the lung expands. This pressure would force fluid, air, or clots out through the drainage tube. Then, when the patient exhales, the pressure in the chest would cease, and the valve tubing would collapse, thereby preventing the air and fluid from backing up.

I wanted to play around with the idea immediately and ran to a nearby five-and-dime store. There, I purchased a Japanese noisemaker that made a sound we used to call a "raspberry" or a "Bronx cheer." The one I picked up had a little plastic mouthpiece attached to a thin piece of flattened rubber or plastic tubing. Blowing through it made that embarrassing noise. Now that I had something I could practice with, I set to work developing my new, retrofitted valve.

A PATIENT RECEIVES THE CHEST DRAIN VALVE

The idea seemed so logical, I wanted to use the flutter valve on a human. About a week after my five-and-dime purchase, a young man was admitted to the hospital with shortness of breath. A chest x-ray showed that one of his lungs had collapsed and his chest was filled with air, the telltale signs of pneumothorax. After obtaining the patient's consent to try the chest drain valve, I gave him local anesthesia and then inserted a tube into his chest. But instead of connecting the tube to the suction apparatus, I attached it to my sterilized flutter-valve device.

I sat at the patient's side for twenty-four hours, observing him carefully. Periodic x-rays showed the flutter valve was working—there was no air trapped in the chest. The valve allowed air to leave the chest while preventing it from getting back in, so the lung could function normally. The patient was breathing and did not have to be tied to a heavy suction apparatus. I felt as though the flutter valve might be the answer I had been seeking.

I took my device to Becton Dickinson and Company in New Jersey, the leading manufacturer of medical equipment. After an extensive series of tests under all kinds of conditions, company researchers determined that the valve stood up. Becton Dickinson made a few dozen devices and called it the Heimlich Chest Drain Valve. I soon started using it on patients who were undergoing chest surgery, including those who had problems relating to the heart, lung, and esophagus. Each time, the chest drain valve worked wonderfully.

THE MILITARY TAKES NOTICE

In January 1966, I spoke at the annual meeting of the American Medical Association in New York City and described a few of the cases where patients had received the chest drain valve and it had worked successfully. After the meeting concluded, four US Navy officers came up to my exhibit. They explained that they were from the National Naval Medical Center (now the Walter Reed National Military Medical Center) in Bethesda, Maryland. The senior officer told me that he was so determined to get Heimlich Chest Drain Valves to Vietnam that he was going to fly to headquarters that day and procure a navy plane, which he would then fly to New York the next day. He asked me to meet him at a nearby airport with six chest drain valves, which he would then immediately take to Vietnam.

The fact that the military was going to be using my valves filled me with joy. It meant that, for the first time in history, a person shot in the chest on the battlefield had a decent chance of surviving.

Shortly after I gave the officer the six Heimlich Chest Drain Valves, I received a telegram from an executive at Becton Dickinson, saying he had received a letter from US Navy lieutenant named Bradley, who wanted one hundred more valves urgently sent to Vietnam. The lieutenant wrote in his letter that he had dropped off the six valves at a medical unit in Vietnam. He continued, "Yesterday I went back and they had used six of them and think they are great. If you could rush 100 more out to us, I think we could have enough data to make a request to get on the supply table."[1] The telegram also said that a commander named Brodine, who headed a naval research unit in Da Nang, believed that the valves were "urgently needed" in Vietnam and were proving to be "a life saving item, and one that the Navy should be interested in ordering as standard items."[2]

The US Air Force also wanted the valves. Becton Dickinson received a letter, dated April 11, 1966, written by a young surgeon who was stationed in Can Tho, Vietnam. As a member of the US Air Force surgical team, Dr. Gerald Baugh treated Vietnamese civilians and soldiers in a building that had once been a hospital but had next to no supplies. According to Dr. Baugh's letter, the injured were "sent to us by helicopter, truck, even ox-carts from miles around." He continued:

One of our greatest difficulties is getting adequate supplies. We see many chest wounds that require immediate closed thoracotomy; we use bladder catheters, rectal tubes, even tubing from our suction machines to accomplish this. There is no adequate way to maintain negative pressure on these devices, and we use simple underwater seals, utilizing any type of bottle we can find.

Last week a member of a sister surgical team out in the field sent us a small number of your No. 420098 B-D Heimlich Chest Drainage Sets. We used them immediately, and both my colleague, a Board Certified Thoracic Surgeon, and myself feel they are the answer to our problems. The few we've used have given uniformly good drainage, and the flutter valve attachment is perfect for our needs.[3]

Dr. Baugh explained that his team was requesting a regular supply of Heimlich Chest Drain Valves from a US medical supplier, but he was so concerned of the time it would take for the devices to reach him in Vietnam that he and a colleague were willing to personally pay Becton Dickinson for them. "We've decided that we would be willing to purchase these tubes, and pay for them out of our salaries, so great is our need for them," he wrote.[4]

The need for the valve was so urgent that even US vice president Hubert Humphrey began to look into the matter. In a letter written to my office and dated July 14, 1966, Humphrey's personal physician, Dr. Edgar F. Berman, said that the vice president had asked him to "investigate the utilization of Heimlich Chest Draining [sic] Valves by the Armed Forces Medical Corps in Vietnam." Dr. Berman stated that the surgeon general's office had noted that more than six hundred of the valves were in Vietnam and "being used for their specific purpose to good avail."[5]

But there was a problem: military bureaucracy. On November 18, 1966, the magazine *Medical World News* published an article titled "Medicine Battles the Odds in Vietnam," which described in heart-wrenching detail the difficulty in saving the lives of soldiers who had been shot in the chest. The article reported that the doctors at a casualty clearing station in Da Nang, Vietnam, suffered "extreme frustration, much of it caused by acute shortages of medical supplies." The doctors cited, as an example, the inability to get Heimlich Chest Drain Valves because the device was not on the official list of medical supplies. When the doctors placed an order for one thousand valves, it took many weeks to get it approved and then more than six months for the valves to be delivered. All the while, countless lives of wounded soldiers were lost.[6]

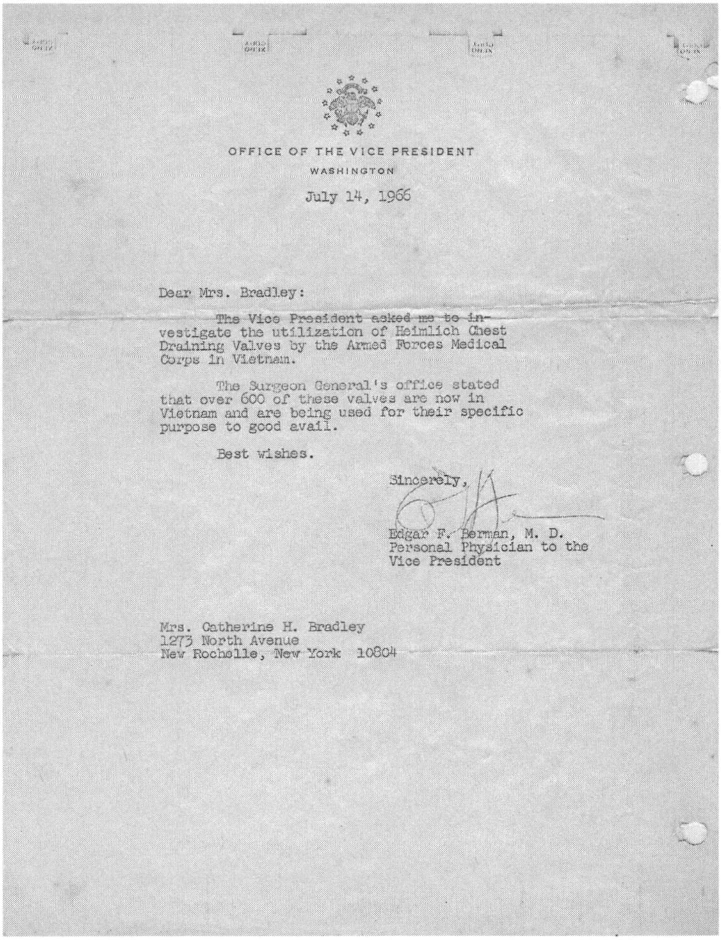

OFFICE OF THE VICE PRESIDENT
WASHINGTON

July 14, 1966

Dear Mrs. Bradley:

The Vice President asked me to investigate the utilization of Heimlich Chest Draining Valves by the Armed Forces Medical Corps in Vietnam.

The Surgeon General's office stated that over 600 of these valves are now in Vietnam and are being used for their specific purpose to good avail.

Best wishes.

Sincerely,

Edgar F. Berman, M. D.
Personal Physician to the
Vice President

Mrs. Catherine H. Bradley
1273 North Avenue
New Rochelle, New York 10804

Figure 11.2. *A request from high up*: When the personal physician of Vice President Hubert Humphrey asked about the Heimlich Chest Drain Valve in 1966, I knew it was badly needed in Vietnam.

Back in the United States, Becton Dickinson was manufacturing the valves as quickly as it could, but the process was slow because the company was making them by hand. In 1964, however, the company was making use of manufacturing assembly lines to get the valves out more quickly. Still, sterilization and quality-control assessment of each valve took weeks.

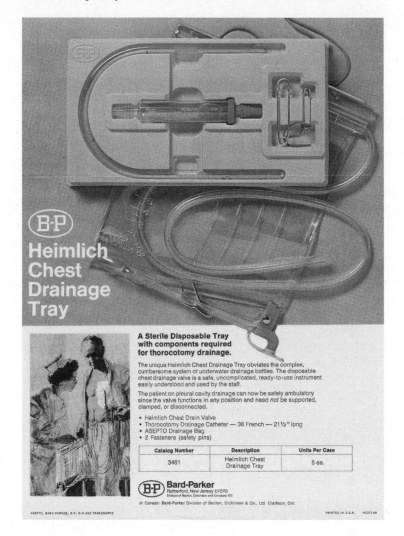

Figure 11.3. *The Heimlich Chest Drain Valve*: A CDV kit used by tens of thousands of soldiers during the Vietnam War and by hundreds of thousands of patients thereafter. (Photograph courtesy of Aspen Surgical and Becton Dickinson.)

Finally, the valves were ready to be shipped to hospitals and to Vietnam. And not a minute too soon, for Becton Dickinson began to receive orders from the military for unlimited quantities. The chest drain valve was such a lifesaver that US soldiers carried them in their packs so that they could save another soldier if he was shot in the chest. And the valves were not only being used on US soldiers. One doctor noted in a letter to me that he was using the valve on Vietnamese civilians. "Their lives are as important to me as any life. We cannot get enough valves," he wrote.

The public was starting to read articles about this device that was saving lives on the other side of the world. I believe these stories gave soldiers and their families hope that they had a better chance of surviving combat. A 1967 article in *Reader's Digest* describes the situation:

> A small device barely five inches long is saving the lives of hundreds of Vietnam wounded—civilian as well as military. Called the Heimlich Chest Drain Valve, the new device, developed by Dr. Henry Heimlich, is used to drain fluids which accumulate in the chest cavity following heart and lung surgery, during certain illnesses, or as a result of a chest wound. Failure to drain can be fatal. The traditional method of draining the chest cavity requires elaborate tubing connected to drainage bottles half-filled with water. . . . Moving the patient with this apparatus, even from one area of a hospital to another, is complicated and often dangerous. Almost insurmountable difficulties arise in combat areas, where the patient must be moved quickly and often. . . . Every soldier carried in a plastic envelope in his pocket a sterile chest tube attached to a Heimlich Valve. If he was shot in the chest, no doctor or nurse was needed. His buddy inserted the drainage tube through the bullet hole and held it in place with a strip of adhesive tape. The wounded soldier was then flown by helicopter to a base camp.[7]

Yet, there were holdups. Families, military personnel, and others complained that the chest drain valves were not getting to the soldiers who needed them. While some blamed the problem on the government and military, in fact, there was such a surge in demand during wartime that the manufacturer simply could not make enough valves to meet the demand. According to Becton Dickinson, the US Army Medical Corps and the US Navy Medical Corps ordered more than twenty thousand Heimlich Chest Drain Valves for use in Vietnam between

1965 and 1968. "We produced the valves running continuously in three shifts to keep the supply flowing to the battlefront," said Ed May in an internal company newsletter.[8] Mr. May was Becton Dickinson's product manager of its Custom and Special Instruments Division at that time.

Since the chest drain valve was so effective in saving lives on the battlefield, I personally made sure that militaries in other countries learned how to use it. When war broke out between Israel and the Arab nations in 1967, I picked up a case of valves from Becton Dickinson and delivered them to Floyd Bennett Field, a naval air station in New York City. From there, a team of Israelis flew them to Tel Aviv.

In 1964, I applied for a patent for the Heimlich Chest Drain Valve. The US Patent Office rejected the application, referencing previous patents for a flutter-type valve designed for other purposes. Five years later, however, the patent office changed its mind and patented the valve on August 26, 1969. At a meeting with my patent lawyer and three patent office attorneys, it was explained to us that the valve had saved so many lives, it deserved a special patent. My patent attorney said he had never seen that happen before.

In the decades following the Vietnam War, the Heimlich Chest Drain Valve has been widely used for any condition requiring chest drainage, not just serious chest injuries and surgery. Doctors have discovered that it helps speed up recovery time and, therefore, reduces cost. Until that time, a patient whose lung had collapsed spent at least two weeks in a hospital bed hooked up to the suction apparatus. Now, when patients go to the emergency room, where a chest tube with a Heimlich valve attached is inserted into the chest, they go home immediately. Two weeks later, the patient returns to the hospital, and the tube is removed.

Dr. Gerald Baugh, the young surgeon in Can Tho, Vietnam, who wrote the letter to Becton Dickinson and was desperate to receive the devices, remembers what it was like to practice medicine in such circumstances. When contacted at his home in Rosanky, Texas, outside Austin, Dr. Baugh explained that he and his team were trying to make do with random tubes they located, sometimes attaching the tubes to soda and beer bottles or to rubber gloves. He was grateful not only to employ the Heimlich Chest Drain Valve in Vietnam but also, after he returned, in the United States when performing chest surgery. Unlike before the device was available, when tubes coming out of a patient's chest were connected to bottles on the floor, the patients now "could get up and walk around, so they had earlier ambulation. I think it gets them well quicker," Dr. Baugh said.

All told, since I invented the device, more than four million Heimlich Chest Drain Valves have saved or improved the lives of soldiers on the battle-field as well as the lives of patients in hospitals, ambulances, and palliative-care settings at the end of life.[9]

Nearly seventy years after that awful day when the Chinese soldier died in my hands at Camp Four, I think that, while I was unable to save him, his death was not in vain, for it motivated me to come up with a solution that saved the lives of so many others.

Figure 11.4. *Gratified*: By the 1960s, my Heimlich Chest Drain Valve was being used to save the lives of soldiers around the world. Today, it is used both in times of war and in hospitals every day.

12

A BOY NAMED HAYANI

In the lives of most doctors, there are those few, special patients whom we remember for the rest of our lives. Mohammed Ben Driss Hayani-Mechkouri was one such patient.

Hayani lived very far from the city of Cincinnati, where my family and I had moved in 1968 and where I had accepted a position as director of surgery at the Jewish Hospital. He was a fourteen-year-old boy of little means and who had suffered greatly throughout his young life. By the time I met Hayani, I had helped many people who had lost the ability to swallow by performing on them the reversed gastric tube operation. And that was exactly the treatment Hayani needed.

But his case was very different than the others. For one, it presented enormous medical challenges due to the severity of his injuries. And two, we got to know each other not only as patient and doctor, but as friends. In some ways, our relationship was like that of father and son.

I first learned about Hayani in the summer of 1970, when I received a letter from a physician in Tangier, Morocco. He explained that Hayani was an orphan living at the Cheshire Foundation Home, a charity institution in Tangier. The Cheshire Foundation had been established by Lord Cheshire, the leading British ace in World War II who had established a string of nearly one hundred foundling homes throughout the Mediterranean area. The young residents of the Tangier facility where Hayani lived were plagued with a litany of afflictions. Some were blind; some, deaf; some, deformed. Many had been found by the Cheshire staff, abandoned in the woods, unable to be cared for by their impoverished parents.

The doctor who wrote to me served in a mission hospital next door to the Cheshire Home and paid visit to the home from time to time. That was how he met Hayani and learned of his condition. The doctor had read about the reversed gastric tube operation and said he believed that Hayani could benefit from it.

A DISASTROUS DRINK

When Hayani was six years old, he suffered a terrible accident. He reached for what he thought was a bottle of soda pop, put it to his lips, and took one long, disastrous swallow of what turned out to be lye. The caustic substance destroyed his esophagus and pharynx, as well as his larynx and vocal cords. Since that time, Hayani had not been able to eat, drink, or speak.

Doctors in Morocco had enabled Hayani to breathe better by performing a tracheotomy, inserting a metal tube through an incision into the trachea. To allow him to consume nutrition, they inserted a feeding tube through his abdomen and into his stomach, into which Hayani poured liquids several times a day. Since he could not swallow his own saliva, he frequently spit it into a cup and drooled onto his pillow at night.

As Hayani got older, he was sent periodically to surgical specialists in the Moroccan capital of Rabat, as well as to France and England. The specialists all said the same thing: restoring normal swallowing was impossible.

The physician who had contacted me about Hayani and I wrote back and forth for several months, during which time we discussed medical, legal, and international matters. By that time, I had been performing the reversed gastric tube operation successfully for well over a decade and had started the Dysphagia Foundation, which raised funds to care for patients afflicted with the inability to swallow. I was hopeful that these funds could be used to underwrite some of the boy's travel and hospital expenses.

I wrote the Moroccan doctor that yes, I would be happy to operate on the boy as soon as the necessary arrangements could be made.

Figure 12.1. *A Cincinnatian*: By the time I met Hayani, I had moved my family to Cincinnati, where I was head of surgery at Jewish Hospital. (Photograph © Sarge Marsh Photo.)

Those arrangements took the rest of the summer and half of the fall. In addition to the money that the Dysphagia Foundation donated, other organizations also contributed, including the London-based Cheshire Foundation. The US consul general in Morocco did away with much red tape and expedited Hayani's passage to America. Air France donated two free flights for Hayani and a nurse to fly from Tangier to Cincinnati.

HAYANI ARRIVES IN CINCINNATI

Hayani arrived in Cincinnati around the middle of October 1970. I met him at the airport, along with a Jewish Hospital nurse, a few hospital officials, and various cameramen and reporters to whom the medical board had issued a press release. Our entourage waited on the tarmac. When the plane door opened, an emaciated, small teenager emerged, followed by the nurse who had accompanied him from Morocco. Both were smiling. When we met, the boy's big eyes shone brightly, although he could not utter a word. Remarkably, Hayani showed no sign of being disoriented, even with all the buzz of attention.

I got Hayani—or "Ben," as many called him—settled into his room at the Jewish Hospital and examined him. Before any surgery could be performed, I conducted some studies to determine his general physical status, which, I was glad to discover, turned out to be pretty good. In addition, an x-ray taken of the stomach (after barium was introduced through the feeding tube) revealed that the stomach had not been severely damaged by the lye. This meant that constructing a reversed gastric tube from the stomach was surgically feasible. Yet there remained two challenges: First, his throat was severely scarred and completely closed high up into the pharynx. I would not know until we operated how challenging it would be to connect the gastric tube to the pharynx. Second, I was unsure if the feeding tube on which Hayani had been relying for many years would interfere with my forming a new, lengthy reversed gastric tube.

During this assessment time, Hayani was well cared for. After his story appeared in the newspapers the day after he arrived, many Cincinnatians visited Hayani in the hospital and brought him enough toys to fill his room. Three members of one prominent family that lived in Tangier and were visiting relatives in Cincinnati made a generous offer. Jean Pierre Francois Joseph Pineton (the marquis de Chambrun, a descendant of the French royal family), his British wife, Bindy, and his sister Marta, Princess Ruspoli of Italy, contacted me after they read about Hayani. Princess Ruspoli explained to me that she and her brother spoke Arabic and would visit Hayani each day. I was thrilled with this idea, and so, from the many months that Hayani stayed in the hospital, one or all of the royal family members spent most every day with Hayani. They played with him and taught him to read and write English.

I OPERATE ON HAYANI

On October 19, 1970, Hayani was wheeled into the operating room. When I opened his abdomen, I could see that the boy's stomach was normal in size and his feeding tube was located in such a way that it would not impede with the construction of the reversed gastric tube. Best of all, the antrum had not been damaged by the lye.

I began to create the reversed gastric tube. Once I had the tube ready, I made a skin-deep incision in the boy's neck. Then I created a tunnel under the skin that extended from the abdominal incision to the neck incision. The purpose of the tunnel was to run the gastric tube through it and up to the neck, thereby creating a cleaner detour free of scar tissue.

However, I did not attempt to connect the newly created esophagus to the pharynx. There was simply too much scarring to contend with, which extended from the lower end of the pharynx all the way to the base of the tongue, the result of both the lye burns and the tracheotomy Hayani had received in Morocco. The final phase of the procedure would need to be done in a second operation. So I closed off the upper end of the gastric tube, ran it through the tunnel under the skin to the incision in the neck. I left Hayani's feeding tube in place; it would be removed once Hayani was eating normally.

The entire procedure took eight hours. During this time, I was standing, hunched over the operating table. In my early years of surgery, I did not take breaks. Sometimes a nurse would bring me a glass of milk or juice that she held up as I drank through a straw. I wanted to keep going, completely focused on my work. (Years later, I learned that it was important to take breaks, and so I would stop operating and eat a sandwich and drink a glass of milk in the surgeons' lounge, then return to the patient wearing a new, sterile gown and rubber gloves.)

On January 7, 1971, three months after Hayani had recuperated from his first operation, he was brought back to the operating room. This time, I was assisted by a prominent ear, nose, and throat surgeon (or otolaryngologist). I reopened the skin incision in the boy's neck, exposing the upper portion of the gastric tube. I was pleased to find that it had healed well.

I opened the upper end of the tube. Then I delicately cut away the scar tissue in the neck area and sewed the end of the tube to the pharynx opening. This was the highest point in the throat to which I had ever connected a reversed gastric tube. Fortunately, the tube stretched easily to the required point. This second operation took about three hours. A few weeks later, Hayani underwent a third operation, during which I removed more scar tissue. The reversed gastric tube was now in place. All that was needed was for Hayani to heal and for him to try to swallow.

STILL UNABLE TO SWALLOW

After replacing Hayani's esophagus with the reversed gastric tube, I was confident we were home free. I expected that within a week or two of surgery, Hayani would be swallowing liquid and food, as my other patients had. But I was in for a disappointment. Nearly a month went by, and Hayani was still unable to swallow either liquids or solids. Every time I tried to feed him anything—even something as bland as milk or gelatin—he would gag and spit it out. We had no choice but to keep feeding him through his stomach tube.

I was confounded. Was there something wrong with the new esophagus I had created? Was the opening between the tube and the pharynx constricted? I measured the size of the opening by passing a large rubber tube through it and discovered that it was large enough for food to pass from the mouth and into the stomach. I looked into the throat through a scope that confirmed the opening was big enough.

I looked for other possible problems. Perhaps the nerves or muscles associated with the swallowing process were defective. If so, nothing could be done to overcome the inability to swallow food. But that was unlikely, I reasoned, since Hayani could open and close his mouth. In any case, gravity would have helped liquids to flow downward. I reviewed medical textbooks on physiologic descriptions of the swallowing process, but these provided no help.

Then, I thought, maybe it wasn't a case of physiology at all. Maybe the switches were all there, but Hayani didn't know how to turn them on.

Maybe Hayani had forgotten how to swallow.

In the newborn infant, sucking and swallowing are reflexes that respond to visualizing food and its presence in the mouth. The tongue and lips grasp the nipple placed in the mouth, and sucking and swallowing reflexively follow. Swallowing becomes a voluntary process, then rapidly becomes a complex and essentially automatic one. But what if someone forgets this innate reflex? The answer is simple: he or she would have to be taught how to get it back. But how? I discussed with other doctors the dilemma; they simply shrugged their shoulders.

But then the director of nursing services at Jewish Hospital gave me the answer. Nurse Isabel Weisman had previously worked in obstetrics and had spent time with newborns who did not have a sucking reflex, such as those born prematurely. When that happens, she said, it's necessary to teach the babies this "instinct," or they will starve. And Nurse Weisman knew just how to do that.

"What you do," I remember her explaining, "is you take the infant's fore-finger, put it in your mouth, and suck it. That way, the baby can feel with its finger the sucking sensation. Then you place that finger in the infant's own mouth. Pretty soon, the infant duplicates the sucking sensation that he felt on his finger. After that, he can do it on his own." Nurse Weisman also taught me that holding the newborn in a sitting position is the most efficient method for helping them eat because gravity helps move the food downward into the stomach.

"You've made my day," I told her and sped off to Hayani's room.

He was sitting in bed. A few friends were visiting. I motioned to Hayani to sit upright in a chair, which he did. Then I asked for his hand and began to suck on his finger. He and his companions must have thought I had lost my mind, but I didn't care. I was determined to teach Hayani how to swallow.

After I had been sucking his finger for a little while, I put that same finger in his mouth and encouraged him to replicate the sucking movements. I couldn't tell if he was getting it, so we kept up this exercise throughout the day, and tried it again the next day, and the next. With each day that went by, Hayani's sucking movement got stronger.

After a week of sucking exercises, I presented Hayani with fluids and gelatin. A nurse sat with us. Hayani raised a spoonful of gelatin to his lips and put it in his mouth. He swallowed, and the gelatin went down. The nurse and I screamed with joy. Hayani smiled broadly as he experienced the act of swallowing for the first time in eight years. He took another spoonful of gelatin. Then another. And another. More smiles.

Over the next few days, Hayani moved on to thicker foods, all served in hospital containers. One morning, as I was on my way to work, I spontaneously stopped at a grocery store and bought a chocolate-covered ice-cream bar on a stick. In my childhood, this had been the treat of all treats—the "Brown Cow" that kids begged their mothers for.

Sitting on the bed with Hayani, I handed him the ice cream. He took it with a puzzled, slightly uneasy look and raised his eyebrows in an expression that said, "Can I?"

I nodded, smiling. Hayani pulled off the wrapper and extracted the pop. Then, hesitantly, holding onto the stick, he raised the ice cream to his mouth, gently licked the chocolate, and took a bite. The chocolate crackled and the vanilla ice cream soon slid across his tongue and down his throat. There was no gagging, no coughing. His face lit up with the biggest smile I have ever seen. In all my years of treating patients, I do not believe I have ever felt more gratified than I did at that moment. Someone snapped a photo of the two of us smiling at each other while Hayani continued to enjoy his treat. Soon after that, Hayani's story was written up in *Medical World News*; the caption that accompanied the photo read: "It's hard to tell who is happier with Hayani's first ice cream—Dr. Heimlich or he."[1]

RELEARNING HOW TO SPEAK

Eating the ice cream pop was a turning point in Hayani's life as a patient. After that, he was able to consume all kinds of foods. Because he was Muslim and could not eat pork, the hospital put him on a kosher diet. After one week, Hayani was eating voraciously.

The next step for Hayani was enabling him to speak. This was a major challenge, given that the lye had eaten away his larynx and vocal cords, but the challenge was admirably met by a speech therapist named Patricia Reading, who taught him a technique known as *esophageal speech*. First, she taught him to swallow air into his stomach and then regurgitate—literally belch—the air.

As the belched air passed the back of his throat and he mouthed words, he was able to clearly emit understandable guttural sounds. This made Hayani unique in the world. To my knowledge, never before had someone whose esophagus and larynx been destroyed produced esophageal speech. Before long, working with Patricia and an English tutor, Hayani could make himself understood, however haltingly, in Arabic, French, and English.

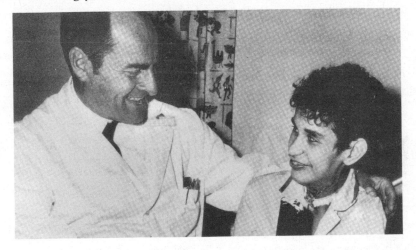

Figure 12.2. *A dear patient*: My memorable "ice-cream moment" for the unforgettable Hayani.

Hayani spent a total of about six months in Cincinnati. During that time, many of those on staff at the hospital had grown fond of him. Nurses, internists, pediatricians, radiologists, and pathologists had all participated in his care at one stage or another. When he was well enough to get around, he was invited to people's homes, where he played with children and spent the night. I had brought him to my home numerous times. My children tell me that they remember how gentle he appeared.

On March 25, 1971, we officially opened the Esophagus Center of the Jewish Hospital, which was devoted specifically to patients with swallowing problems. When I was handed the scissors to be used to cut the ceremonial ribbon, I looked down at Hayani and handed the scissors to him, and he proudly gave the ribbon a snip. *Medical World News* described the scene this way: "When it came to the question of who should cut the ribbon at the dedication of the new esophagus center, there was only one candidate. Hayani may not understand the dilatation and diagnosis that will go on in the three-bed unit or comprehend the endoscopy and motility studies that will take place. . . . But no one knows better than he what the center is for: He can swallow again, and he has friends."[2]

The day Hayani went back to Morocco, many tears were shed—tears of sorrow by those who would miss him and tears of joy for having known, admired, and loved this brave young man.

A VISIT TO MOROCCO

When Hayani left in March, I didn't expect to see him ever again. But later that year, in appreciation for my efforts on the boy's behalf, King Hassan II of Morocco invited Jane and me to visit. Before arriving in Tangier, we wondered what it was like for Hayani to be back at the Cheshire Foundation Home after having been the focus of so much loving attention while in Cincinnati. Was he still eating and drinking? Was he still speaking?

When Jane and I saw Hayani, he looked as happy as could be. Since he'd been back, he'd been spending time with the other children living in the home. He had also become employed at the hospital next door, working in the x-ray department.

Observing the other children being cared for at the home was a sobering experience. Many were deformed. One young boy, whose legs were stretched rigidly out behind him, virtually "ran" around the grounds on his hands. But their joyful expressions and the good-heartedness of those who cared for them warmed our hearts.

Jane and I brought Hayani to our hotel and treated him to lunch. We were once again charmed by his infectious smile and apparent ability to seem at home in the most unfamiliar circumstances. The hotel staff, who all knew Hayani's story from newspaper reports, treated us grandly.

We were pleased to see Hayani eating perfectly normally. Jane described this trip in an article she wrote for the *Cincinnati Post*, published on October 19, 1972: "At lunch, our first day in Tangier, my husband and I watched Hayani spear the last French fry on his plate. Except for the operative scars on his neck, our 16-year-old companion with his thatch of curly black hair, trace of a moustache, looked the picture of health."[3]

But Jane continues, "Our pleasure in seeing Hayani do justice to his meal was dimmed by the discovery that he had forgotten how to speak. Initially, our conversation centered around Hayani, but my husband and I soon began talking to one another. Suddenly, we heard a faint sob, and, turning back to Hayani, saw that he was crying."[4]

During the three days Hayani stayed with us at the hotel, I made several attempts to induce him to speak.

"Watch what I do," I said. I then sipped some carbonated mineral water and then burped "hel-lo," just as Hayani had been taught in the hospital.

"Now you try it," I said, pouring some water in another glass. Hayani sadly shook his head. I recapped the bottle. "You'll be talking by the time we leave," I said cheerfully.

On our last day in Tangier, we are having lunch with Hayani when I had an idea. "What do you do at the hospital?"

Hayani quickly pantomimed the *click-click* motion of operating the camera. "No; tell me," I said, pointing to Hayani's carbonated soda drink, but he sat motionless, his eyes downcast.

"How many hours do you work?" I persisted. I put my face close to Hayani's. "Tell me: How many hours do you work?"

Hayani rolled his eyes helplessly. Then he took a swallow of soda. His face contorted with the struggle to speak.

"Three," he belched.

I continued the questioning. "And what do you do at the hospital?"

Another swallow. A pause. "X-ray."

The waiter came to take dessert orders. I smiled, remembering the success that followed his ice-cream pop in the hospital. "Will you have ice cream?" I asked. Hayani nodded. Not letting him off that easily, I said, "What kind would you like?"

Hayani motioned for the waiter to be patient. Then, after a short while, he said, "Chocolate."

We spent a week in Tangier. Before we left to go back home, Jane and I visited the Cheshire Foundation Home and had one last opportunity to see Hayani. Outside the gate, we shook hands with him and several officials of the house.

"Remember," I said to Hayani, smiling, "if you're coming back to Cincinnati, you must talk." Hayani nodded and swallowed forcibly as he prepared to utter the last words he would ever say to me.

"Good bye, Doctor."

Shortly after our visit, Morocco underwent a series of political upheavals that resulted in the institution of a more traditional Islamic government and the expulsion of French residents, including doctors who had been practicing there for decades. In this new environment, medical standards rapidly deteriorated, and many Moroccans, whom Western science might have saved, succumbed to disease. Tragically, Hayani was one of those individuals. I found out from one of his friends that Hayani had died of pneumonia at the age of twenty-one.

Yet Hayani's memory stays with me. I could never forget his calm demeanor, sense of humor, and contagious smile. And he has another legacy, too. Shortly after I helped Hayani regain his ability to swallow, I began using the same technique with other patients who also needed to relearn the act of swallowing. It was a valuable teaching method that grew out of an unforgettable ice-cream moment shared by me and one bright-eyed Moroccan teenage boy.

13

SAVING THE LIVES OF CHOKING VICTIMS: THE HEIMLICH MANEUVER

Here's a question to ponder: What do President Ronald Reagan; actors Elizabeth Taylor, Goldie Hawn, Jack Lemmon, Cher, Carrie Fisher, Ellen Barkin, Nicole Kidman and Halle Berry; basketball sportscaster Dick Vitale; famed cookbook writer Joan Nathan; Mayor Ed Koch; and newsman John Chancellor all have in common?[1]

Answer: Each choked on food and were saved with something I invented called the *Heimlich Maneuver*.

Many people ask me how I came up with it. Sometimes people guess that it came about by accident. Was I standing next to someone who was choking and I accidentally bumped into the person, causing the food in the throat to shoot out?

I assure you, the process of coming up with the maneuver was much more methodical than that. In fact, I invented it just as I have all my other techniques and devices—that is, through scientific research.

CHOKING: A SERIOUS PROBLEM

I first became interested in the problem of choking in 1972. I was sitting in our kitchen in Cincinnati, reading an article in the *New York Times* Sunday magazine about accidental deaths. My wife, Jane, was in the room with me. I read aloud to her the article citing the top causes of accidental deaths. Most would be what you would expect: car accidents, fire, drowning, and falls.

What caught my eye was the sixth leading cause of accidental death—it was choking on food or a foreign object. Nearly four thousand people were dying from choking each year in this country alone. Most commonly, people choked to death on a piece of food, or, with children, a small object they had put in their mouths. What's more, choking was the number-one cause of accidental death in the home for children under the age of one.

What is particularly frightening is that, when someone is choking, it takes only four minutes before the person dies or suffers permanent brain damage.

After my many years of working to solve problems related to the esophagus, this sobering news seemed right up my alley, so I began to look into what we knew about how to save chocking victims.

I reviewed the medical literature and learned that it discussed three different kinds of procedures. The first kind involved creating an opening in the trachea to make a temporary airway. The second required external devices used to remove the object. And the third was hitting the choking victim on the back.

The first type of treatment involved inserting a large-caliber hypodermic needle into the trachea or performing a tracheotomy. The latter method involved making a slit in the neck, usually with a knife, to create a breathing hole in the trachea. Both of these methods were dangerous and could hardly be performed by a layperson outside of a hospital. In fact, I recall reading about a physician who tried to save his wife, who was choking, by performing a tracheotomy on her with a kitchen knife. He literally slit her throat—he cut her carotid artery—and she died of a hemorrhage.

Some medical researchers were coming up with instruments that were designed to remove the object from the throat. There was the Throat-E-Vac, an apparatus that used suction to remove the object. One medical researcher was trying to market a pair of nine-inch-long plastic tweezers called the "choke-saver," designed to slip down the victim's throat and grasp the blocking food. The drawbacks of such devices are obvious: They require that such instruments be handy in the unexpected instance that a person chokes. And it would be virtually impossible for choking victims to use these devices on themselves.

Slapping choking victims on the back was a commonly used method. However, I could find little or no scientific basis for the efficacy of back slaps.

What's more, people who were only partially choking—meaning they were still able to breathe to some extent—risked having the object be driven more deeply into the airway if they were slapped on the back.

So my research told me what *not* to do if someone chokes, but what was the solution? Then I began thinking: maybe the current methods were approaching the problem from the wrong end.

With both the tracheotomy and the back slaps, people tried to save someone from choking by doing something above the blocked airway. What about attacking the problem from *below* the blockage? As a thoracic surgeon, I knew there is always residual air left in the lungs, even after forcibly breathing out. When a person exhales normally, there is residual air left in the lungs that measures between 1.8 to 2.4 liters. If there was a way to make use of this air, would it be enough to expel a trapped object in an individual's airway? I thought about how a pair of bellows works to blow air into a fire. The air is expelled when one compresses the bellows. Could a person's lungs be compressed in the same way?

A SUCCESSFUL EXPERIMENT

In 1973, I decided to try to answer this question by setting up an experiment in my laboratory at Cincinnati's Jewish Hospital, where I was the director of surgery. I used an eight-inch-long endotracheal tube with a diameter the size of a nickel and a balloon wrapped around one end. I sealed one end of the tube to prevent air from getting through and inserted it into the airway of an anaesthetized dog. I then inflated the balloon, figuring it would act like a foreign object and obstruct the dog's airway. If I could produce a large enough flow of air by compressing the lungs, the tube should be expelled from the airway.

Once I inflated the balloon, the dog stopped breathing, signaling that he was choking. Immediately, I pressed on the dog's chest, but the tube did not move. I tried it again. Still, the tube went nowhere. I tried it a few more times and still no results. I quickly removed the tube, and the dog began to breathe again.

I stopped to analyze the situation. Obviously, simply pushing on the chest did not compress the lungs sufficiently. The problem was the rib cage—the rigid, bony ribs held their shape under extreme pressure. After all, from an evolutionary standpoint, that is the purpose of the ribs, to protect the body against a blow to the heart and other vital organs.

I moved down the body in my thinking and thought about the diaphragm, the flat muscle that separates the chest from the abdomen. If I pushed the diaphragm upward into the chest, perhaps that would create the "bellows" effect and force air from the lungs upward, expelling the tube out of the dog's throat.

I turned back to my sleeping, canine patient, and I again inserted the tube and inflated the balloon until the dog began to choke. Then I placed my fist on the dog's belly, just under the rib cage, and pushed the diaphragm upward into the chest.

Instantly, the tube shot out of the animal's mouth.

Once I got over the shock, I repeated the procedure. I again induced choking and pushed upward on the dog's diaphragm. Again, the tube flew out of the dog's mouth. I tried it a few more times, and each time, I got the same result. In trying different amounts of pressure, I also discovered that this same effect was achieved even when I applied only a little bit of pressure.

I sent my assistant down to the hospital cafeteria for a piece of meat. When he returned, I put the meat into the anesthetized animal's windpipe, knowing I could pull it out if my method failed. I again pressed the chest (rather than the diaphragm this time) repeatedly. Nothing happened. Then I moved my hands just below the rib cage and pressed upward on the diaphragm. As with the tube, the meat shot out of the dog's mouth. I repeated the procedure over and over. Each time, my pushes expelled the meat.

I wondered what would happen if I applied the same pushes in the case of a partial blockage. At first, I thought the method would not work, that the object would have to be stuck tightly in the windpipe, like a champagne cork in a bottle, to allow enough pressure to build up and pop out the meat. But as I experimented, I found that the flow of air past an object only partially obstructing the trachea, like a chicken bone, was still enough to push the object upward and out of the mouth. *It was the flow of air, not the amount of pressure, that carried the object away.*

I went about measuring the actual measure of airflow. Working with my fellow doctors and some hospital residents, we calculated the airflow quite easily with some simple tests. Each of us was fitted with a mouthpiece that was connected by tubing to a machine that measured the flow of air passing out of our mouths. We then let our colleagues force our diaphragms upward using their fists. Today, the results would be measured by a computer, but in our day, it was measured by a graph on a rotating drum.

The figures were astounding. During normal breathing, a person exhales about two gallons of air per minute. But when we forced our diaphragms upward with a fist, each application of the method produced almost a *quart* of air in one-quarter of a second. This force of air came to *almost 60 gallons of air per minute*, more than enough to drive a trapped object out of the throat.

I initially dubbed my method "sub-diaphragmatic pressure." It would take a while before it received a catchier name.

USING AIR IN THE LUNGS TO PUSH OUT AN OBJECT

I had proved one important thing: pushing in and up on the diaphragm—at a point just above the navel and below the ribs—creates a flow of air from the lungs that can expel an object out of the airway. Now I just had to figure out how best to go about creating that "push." The technique had to be simple enough so that anyone could apply it quickly. I was reminded of the scary fact that brain damage and death are only minutes away. I knew there was no time for people to depend on a household instrument to perform the "pushing" technique. What if the device was not handy at the time it was needed? Paramedics would not be of much good, since they would most likely not arrive in time to save the person's life.

I tossed around some ideas. What procedure would be simple enough for anyone to understand, even a child? What procedure would be easy enough for anyone to perform in any situation? I came up with several possible options. For example, a person could brace the victim's back against a wall and push with a fist against the upper abdomen. Or a person could lay the victim on the ground and push with a hand or foot on the upper abdomen. I tried these different methods on some friends. Finally, I settled on these five simple steps:

1. Stand behind the victim and reach around the person's waist with both arms.
2. Make a fist with one hand.
3. Place the thumb side of your fist below the rib cage, just above the belly button.
4. Grasp the fist with your other hand and press the fist inward and upward.
5. Perform the technique firmly and repeat it until the choking object is dislodged from the airway.

In addition to this basic method, I investigated how to apply the technique in different situations. For example, suppose a person faced a choking victim of such large stature that the rescuer could not reach around the victim's waist. Suppose a small woman or a child was trying to save a large man. What would happen if the victim had lost consciousness and had fallen to the floor? Was it necessary to lift the victim to a standing position? What if he or she was too heavy?

To plan for these contingencies, I developed an alternate, lying-down position. With the victim lying down on his back, the rescuer kneels astride the victim's thighs, facing him. Then she places one hand on top of the other and puts the heel of the bottom hand on the same spot, just above the belly button and under the rib cage. The rescuer can use her body weight to overcome the size differential. In this way, a smaller individual could likely save a large or overweight person. Even a very young child might be able to save an adult.

By 1974, about one year after I had begun my experiments, I believed my technique could save lives and that I had enough evidence to introduce it to the public. But I knew the clock was ticking. People were choking to death every day. Usually, the way medical solutions become popularized is by performing time-consuming studies in hopes that the findings are published in a prestigious medical journal. This could take months or years. How many people might choke to death in that time? I was anxious to educate the entire country as soon as possible.

I decided that I would use the media to tell others about my discovery.

GETTING THE WORD OUT

The idea of using the press to get the word out about my antichoking method was highly unorthodox for 1974. Back then, not only did researchers tend to go the medical-journal route, but also doctors, hospitals, clinics, and drug companies did not advertise themselves and their products directly to the public as they do today. In fact, using the popular media to disseminate health information was discouraged by the medical establishment, and doctors generally considered it unethical to talk to the press.

But I decided I would disregard the accepted attitude. Lives were at stake, and I believed that using the media was the fastest way to allow others to learn about my method and put it to use.

I first approached *Emergency Medicine*, a medical journal that had published some of my previous work. I called the editor and said that I'd like him to publish an article of mine about a technique I had devised for saving the lives of choking persons, and he agreed.

"Pop Goes the Café Coronary" appeared in *Emergency Medicine* in June 1974. (The term "Café Coronary" refers to the fact that people frequently choke to death while eating in a restaurant, while onlookers often mistakenly assume that the person is having a heart attack. That year, I developed what became a universal symbol for choking—holding your hand around your throat—to allow the victim to communicate, "I'm choking.") In the article, I make clear that my experiments had been used only on dogs. "We cannot be certain, of course, that the experimental results will be duplicated in humans," I wrote. "Only by disseminating public information about this simple technique can we determine whether it will result in a significant reduction of what amounts to 3900 totally avoidable deaths every year."[2]

I had asked the editor of *Emergency Medicine* to send the article to syndicated medical columnist Arthur Snider, who had reported on my reversed gastric tube operation twenty years earlier. On June 16, 1974, Mr. Snider's column—carrying the headline, "A New Method to Save Food-Chokers"—began appearing in hundreds of newspapers across the country.[3]

One week later, this headline appeared on the front page of the *Seattle Times*: "News Article Helps Prevent a Choking Death." Someone had read Mr. Snider's column and had tried my technique on a choking person. And it had worked.

Figures 13.1–3. *The Heimlich Maneuver*: There are various ways the Heimlich Maneuver can be performed, depending on the size of the victim, the size of the rescuer, and whether the victim has collapsed.

These medical illustrations were originally created by renowned surgeon and artist Dr. Frank H. Netter.

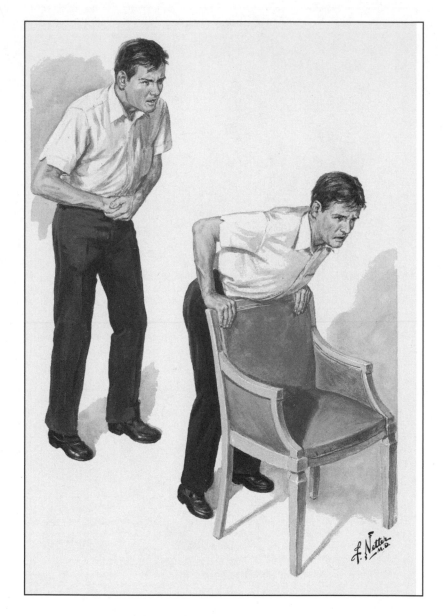

(Netter illustrations used with permission of Elsevier, Inc. All rights reserved. www.netterimages.com.)

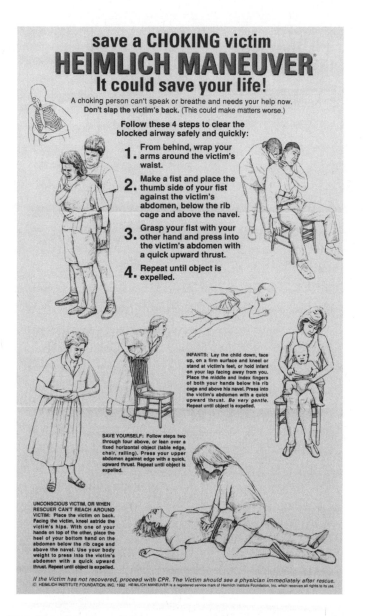

Figure 13.4. *Teaching tool*: As restaurants put up posters on how to do the Heimlich Maneuver, staff were able to jump into action and save lives. (Image courtesy of Deaconess Associations, Inc.)

THE FIRST SAVE

Isaac Piha was sitting in his cabin on Hood Canal when he read about my method in the *Seattle Times*. Piha was particularly interested because he was a retired restaurateur who had seen several of his patrons choke to death on pieces of meat. A few days after reading the article, Piha was enjoying a Father's Day gathering when he heard a neighbor named Edward Bogachus calling for help. Piha and his family ran to the Bogachuses' cabin, where they found Mrs. Bogachus slumped at the dinner table and turning blue (choking victims turn blue from a lack of oxygen in the blood).

"I thought about heart attack and about that article in the *Times* while I was running to the cabin," Piha was quoted saying. "When I saw that they'd been eating dinner, I knew it was food lodged in her throat."[4]

Piha performed my technique on Mrs. Bogachus, which dislodged a large piece of chicken from her throat, and she quickly recovered. To my knowledge, Mr. Piha is the first person to have performed on a human choking victim what later became known as the Heimlich Maneuver.

It did not take long before I heard of another save, and another, and so on. People began saving the lives of their children, their spouses, and strangers in restaurants. Children became rescuers, too. Young people saved adults and sometimes other children. For instance, I remember reading about a four-year-old girl who saved the life of her two-year-old brother when he was choking on a piece of chicken. The boy was eating in his high chair. After he became silent and started turning blue, the girl got behind the high chair and performed the technique. A large piece of chicken skin flew out of the two-year-old's mouth. The girl had learned the technique from watching family members practice it. (Ten years later, at a ceremony recognizing those who had saved the lives of children, I presented a letter of congratulations to the girl—by then, a teenager—and stated that she was the youngest in the world to have ever successfully used the Heimlich Maneuver to save the life of a choking victim.[5])

That life saved in Salt Lake City showed that if a four-year-old can do the technique, anyone can.

I recall the director of medical services at the Albert Einstein Medical Center in Philadelphia telling me how his wife started choking on a chicken bone at a dinner party. The bone—one and a half inches long and pointed at both ends—did not completely block her airway. After two application of the technique, the bone flew out of the woman's mouth. This report confirmed what my experiments had demonstrated: It was not necessary for an object to completely block the airway for the technique to work. Even an object like a bone or a toothpick, which allows a flow of air around it, can be dislodged with my method.

WHEN THE CHOKING VICTIM IS ALONE

The stories continued to come in. People reported saving their relatives, next-door neighbors, spouses, even pets. Then I received a letter in 1975 from Luvan Troendle, a woman in Minnesota who reported a most unusual and significant case—one that occurred years before I invented my antichoking method but that eventually led to me coming up with additional instructions for employing my technique.

"You must have received hundreds of letters about your 'Heimlich Hug' but this one has a different tack," the letter said. Troendle explained that she and her husband had been vacationing in Canada in 1959 with two other couples. One night, while she was inside a cabin with the group and her husband was outside cleaning fish, the host served up steaks. "I was trying to chew my steak which was very tough but I could not chew it into small pieces and I would not dare to spit it out so I decided to swallow it . . . but it stuck in my throat!"

Troendle wrote that she then left the table. "I knew I could never explain to the liquor-happy diners what had happened! My only hope was to get to the door and summon my husband but when I got across the twenty feet of the cabin floor and opened the door I knew I could never call to my husband . . . and I would not be able to explain if I did get his attention. My breath was failing and I knew I could not run the fifty feet to the boat dock where he had been cleaning fish.

"I decided to do the only thing available . . . to give myself a 'thump' on the back . . . so-to-speak . . . and I threw myself against the handrail of the cabin stoop. The most astonishing thing happened!!! The piece of steak flew out of my mouth and landed on the ground eight feet away! I had saved a life with this act . . . <u>my own!</u>"

She went on to say that the incident taught her something important: "<u>I could help myself</u> . . . AND I could help someone else in a similar plight." On the back of the letter, she had drawn a rough sketch of what happened when she saved her own life.

Figure 13.5. *Solo save*: People have saved themselves from choking by performing the Heimlich Maneuver on themselves in creative ways. Luvan Troendle wrote me a letter including this sketch, describing how she saved herself. (Sketch by Luvan Troendle.)

There were other reports of solo saves. I heard of a woman who was choking and who saved herself by pushing into her upper abdomen with her own fist, for example. (In 1983, the *Journal of the American Medical Association*, or *JAMA*, published a letter to the editor, written by a physician in Bethesda, Maryland, who stated that he had saved himself the same way. Dr. Thomas Carlile wrote that his airway was cut off by a pill. "I instinctively clasped my left wrist with my right hand and forced them vigorously into the substernal region. The tablet was forcefully expelled across the small bathroom and shattered on the lavatory mirror into a powder."[6]) I soon realized that people could save themselves by finding a number of creative ways to press up on their diaphragms, such as pressing against the edge of a table, the back of a chair, the edge of a sink, or any other firm object.

But regardless of how people chose to save others and themselves from choking, my method was working. People who would have otherwise died from choking were alive. A letter written to me on November 11, 1975, captured this feeling. It came from Frank Wicher, an attorney in Sioux City, Iowa, who was blind. Mr. Wicher explained that he and his wife were having a steak dinner at a large table with ten people present.

"There appeared to be a little commotion across the table from me and the folks informed me that my wife was choking." Once he realized this, Mr. Wicher "whipped around that table as fast as a man might who could see" and performed my technique on her, once, twice, three times. "The chunk of unchewed steak was ejected and she was breathing once again," he wrote. "I know full well, Dr. Heimlich, that had I not read of your procedure I would have buried my wife six months ago. . . . From the bottom of our hearts, my wife and I thank you. My six daughters thank you as do our eleven grandchildren."

A short time later, Mr. Wicher arranged for me to go to Sioux City, and we had lunch in the restaurant where he had saved his wife.

MY PROCEDURE GETS A NAME

While developing and refining the technique, I had given little thought to what it should be called. Then, two months after the first article appeared in *Emergency Medicine*, I received a phone call from an editor of *JAMA*.

Because my procedure had saved many lives, he felt it should be given a name and that it should be named after me.

"We don't know whether to call it the Heimlich Method or Heimlich Maneuver," he said. "A maneuver is something done once, or the same procedure is repeated. A method is a series of steps, like a urine analysis."

I did not want to spend the rest of my life explaining how my work was like a urine analysis.

"Maneuver!" I shouted into the phone. In an August 12, 1974, editorial, *JAMA* editors described my procedure as the "Heimlich Maneuver."[7] It was the first time that the name was made public.

Soon after the editorial was published, I received a letter from *JAMA*'s editor in chief, asking me to write an article describing my discovery. My article, "A Life-Saving Maneuver to Prevent Food-Choking," was published in the October 1975 issue of *JAMA*.[8] When the article appeared, there was an accompanying editorial stating that the Heimlich Maneuver had been officially endorsed by the Commission on Emergency Medical Services of the American Medical Association, the country's foremost medical organization. The editorial stated that the maneuver is "a most important addition to the emergency care procedures for the person choking on food or other objects that shut off the airway."[9]

THE MANEUVER GOES MAINSTREAM

The maneuver was also catching on outside the medical community. Before I knew it, the technique was making its way into the scripts of soap operas, sitcoms, game shows, and films. Many comedians made light of how people could save a life by wrapping one's arms around a choking victim. Movie director Woody Allen wrote a comical short story titled "A Giant Step for Mankind," which chronicles the desperate attempts by three obscure scientists who are determined to discover a technique to save people from choking. The three experiment with water and tweezers, induce choking in mice, and seek out choking victims in restaurants.[10]

I appeared on such radio and television talk programs as the *Today* show, *Good Morning America*, and, my favorite, *The Tonight Show Starring Johnny Carson*.

My name and that of my technique became household words. In 1979, *Life* magazine published new words of the decade. One of them was *Heimlich Maneuver*.[11] Then, shortly after the new year began, I received a copy of the

Random House Dictionary from its publisher. There, on page 887, was the definition of *Heimlich Maneuver*.

I was amused to discover that my name had become a verb in the American lexicon. People would say, "I did the 'Heimlich' on him," or "I 'Heimliched' her." The term *Heimlich Maneuver* was translated into countless languages such as Spanish (as *Maniobra de Heimlich*) and German (as *Heimlich-Handgriff*).

It made me happy to see that the public was becoming more and more aware of the maneuver for one simple reason: getting the word out—to have the technique become part of our culture—increased the possibility that people would learn how to do the maneuver and use it to save lives.

The maneuver helped to create an image of me as a doctor who was an authority in any emergency situation. In the late 1970s, I initiated discussions with the ABC network about producing a cartoon that would teach children medical first aid. The cartoon—which was to air on Saturday mornings during children's programming—would feature me as a goofy, bald character in a white lab coat who pops up on the screen amid a medical crisis, offering advice. "HELP! Dr. Henry's Emergency Lessons for People" became a series of six, one-minute animated segments that taught kids what to do in such emergency situations as a cut finger or drowning. In 1979, "HELP!" won an Emmy Award for best children's show. During that time, children recognized me as "Dr. Henry," the character who suddenly appeared in the cartoon to guide children through dealing with an emergency. In 1980, Simon and Schuster published a book called *Dr. Heimlich's Home Guide to Emergency Medical Situations*. I was thrilled to cowrite the book with Lawrence Galton, the acclaimed medical writer who had written for *Cosmopolitan* about the case of Virginia Dixon.

As a physician who never imagined that my work would ever catapult me into fame, it was difficult sometimes to comprehend being known to millions of people around the world. But once I accepted what was happening, I realized that I was grateful for the attention the maneuver received, for it meant that those millions of people were learning how to recognize when people were choking and how to save them.

Figure 13.6. *The maneuver, Jane, and me*: Jane and I pose in a "maneuver" embrace for *People* magazine in 1999. (Photograph reproduced by permission from Black/Toby.)

To this day, I continue to read articles on a daily basis of people who have been saved with the maneuver. Around Christmastime 2012, eleven-year-old Louis Fritz of Cincinnati, where I reside, saved his eight-year-old brother, Davis, when he was choking on orange slices. Louis performed the maneuver on Davis three times until the food popped out and landed on the family's kitchen table.[12] I had the honor of meeting young Louis at his school when I presented him with a Heimlich Institute Certificate of Heroism Award.

Figure 13.7. *A simple lifesaver*: The Heimlich Maneuver became famous worldwide because of its simplicity and effectiveness.

The Heimlich Maneuver became popular for one simple reason: it allows anyone—no matter how small or how old—to save a life. Furthermore, the maneuver is easy to learn, it's easy to use, and it's effective. Of course, there is always the possibility that well-meaning people will injure choking victims in the process of trying to save them. Injuries can occur when the maneuver is applied incorrectly, but they are often relatively minor, considering the person was saved from choking to death.

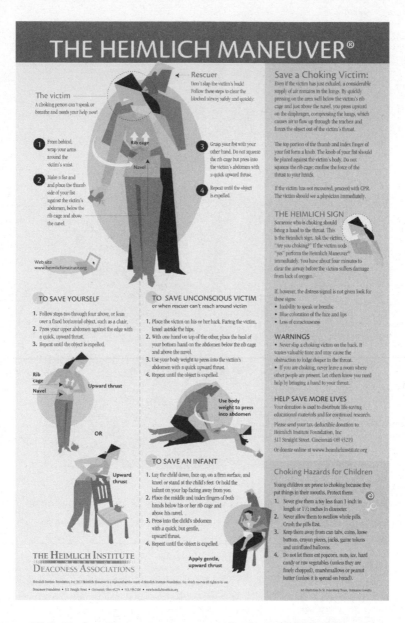

Figure 13.8. *Today*: Restaurants across the United States hang a poster showing staff how to perform the Heimlich Maneuver. These posters are invaluable because servers often save the lives of choking victims. (Image courtesy of Deaconess Associations, Inc.)

Yet, despite all the success the Heimlich Maneuver has achieved—and the thousands of lives saved—one large first-aid organization has historically rejected the technique while insisting on teaching people another method that has an abysmal track record of saving a choking person. My battle to convince this organization to correct its mistake has proven to be one of the fiercest struggles of my life.

14

THE AMERICAN RED CROSS
AND BACK BLOWS

In 1978, a mother sued the Harrisburg, Pennsylvania, school system for not having properly trained its staff on how to save children from choking. A few years before, the woman's son, Gary Daniels, was eating a peanut butter sandwich at school and started choking. A teacher began slapping Gary on the back. The boy continued to choke and fell unconscious. Apparently, the food was not completely blocking his windpipe, because he did not die immediately.[1]

But Gary Daniels never woke up after that. Having been denied oxygen for several minutes, he suffered severe brain damage, lapsed into a coma, and died a few years later.

I became an expert witness in the case.

When contacted on July 19, 2013, Richard Angino, the attorney who represented Gary's mother, said he remembered the case well because of the emotional aspect of it.

"We were all moved by this case," said Mr. Angino, "because this wonderful mother had taken care of her son for years at home. She deserves a place in heaven."

Speaking from his law office in Harrisburg, Mr. Angino remembered explaining to the jury that the school was to blame for failing to teach the staff on how to do the Heimlich Maneuver. The case was settled out of court for $325,000.

"Nobody fought me on the fact that if the teacher had done the Heimlich Maneuver, the boy would not be in a coma," said Mr. Angino.

The case of Gary Daniels is not an isolated one. I have known from the time I conducted my research on the maneuver that back slaps were ineffective in expelling an object from someone's windpipe. But I also believe that they are dangerous, based on numerous cases and studies showing that back slaps not only failed to dislodge an object but also drove an object that was partially blocking the airway deeper into the throat to the point at which the airway was then completely blocked.

On the other hand, the Heimlich Maneuver, when performed correctly, is safe and saves lives. When I invented it in 1974, cases poured in from around the world from people who had saved someone's life or who had had his or her own life saved. A 1985 French study showed that the maneuver could be successfully used in very young children and infants.[2] It's clear that the maneuver is the best solution for virtually any choking victim, adults and children alike.

So I was astonished to discover that the nation's premier first-aid organization, the American Red Cross, was teaching people to hit choking victims on the back.

TEACHING A POTENTIALLY DANGEROUS METHOD

The American Red Cross was founded in 1881 by medical pioneer Clara Barton; it was issued as a corporate charter by the US Congress in 1905. Under the charter, the Red Cross has three main responsibilities: (1) to fulfill the provisions of the Geneva Conventions, (2) to provide family communications and other forms of support to the US military, and (3) to maintain a system of domestic and international disaster relief, including mandated responsibilities under the National Response Framework coordinated by the Federal Emergency Management Agency (FEMA).[3]

Today, the organization is a lifesaving behemoth. It has a national network of more than 769 regional or city chapters. It mobilizes more than one million volunteers each year and has on staff forty thousand employees to provide relief to people affected by natural disasters worldwide.[4] It trains some nine million people in necessary medical skills each year[5] and wields enormous influence over the distribution of medical information in the United States.

Supported by donations and the sales of blood products and educational materials, the Red Cross operates on a $4.1 billion budget.[6]

The Red Cross began recommending that people hit choking victims on the back in 1933. Over time, medical authorities grew to question whether back slaps were effective and safe. In 1969, the American Broncho-Esophagological Association warned that back slaps are dangerous.[7] Following that advice, the Red Cross told people *not* to use back slaps. From 1973 to 1978, the organization stated the following in its teaching manuals: "Do not allow anyone to slap you on your back if you choke . . . except as a last, desperate effort to save his life."[8]

Then came the Heimlich Maneuver in 1974. As soon as the discovery became known, individuals began trying it, and it was not long before reports of people saving the lives of others—as well as their own lives—began to pour in. Many times, people who had witnessed the incidents described how objects "flew" out of victims' mouths. In October 1975, the American Medical Association Commission on Emergency Medical Services endorsed the Heimlich Maneuver as "a most important addition" to other antichoking methods.[9]

Meanwhile, hitting a choking victim on the back became less and less popular as the method of choice. Two years after the maneuver became known, a study published in the *Journal of the American College of Emergency Physicians* (*JACEP*) that measured airflow generated from applying pressure to various parts of the body showed that back slaps were ineffective at creating airflow—airflow that would be needed to dislodge an object caught in the windpipe. Researchers concluded, "The technique of delivering a sharp blow between the shoulder blades . . . was so ineffective in creating airflow or increased pressure within the chest, it was abandoned."[10]

Given what we knew about the effectiveness of the Heimlich Maneuver and the problems related to back slaps, one might think that the Red Cross felt justified with its decision to stop teaching the back slap. Yet in 1976, the Red Cross inexplicably changed its policies, advocating that people use *both* back slaps and what it called "abdominal thrusts." By "abdominal thrust," the organization meant the Heimlich Maneuver. The reason why they didn't refer to the technique as such is because I refused to allow them to use my name. I knew that hitting choking victims on the back was a bad idea and didn't want my name associated with the organization's teachings.[11] Thus, the organization came up with the term *abdominal thrust*. (The Red Cross has made a bad situation worse, however, by using that term because it gives the impression that one can press anywhere on the abdomen, and this has the potential to cause abdominal injuries and fail to save a choking victim.)

WEAK EVIDENCE

I learned about the organization's position shift at a meeting with Red Cross and National Academy of Sciences officials in Chicago that year. Dr. Archer Gordon, who was a physician and who served as a leading advisor on choking to the Red Cross, described at the meeting two unpublished studies he had conducted that led him to conclude that back slaps effectively saved people from choking to death. Dr. Gordon explained that he had taken four anesthetized baboons, put a piece of meat in each of their throats, and hit them on the back. With that blow, he claimed, the meat had then been "loosened."[12]

In the second study, Dr. Gordon explained that he had anesthetized six human volunteers and placed pieces of meat in their throats, just as he had with the baboons. In the human study, the physician explained that he had tied a string to the meat so that it could be pulled out, if necessary. According to Dr. Gordon, back slaps were administered to the subjects, after which the meat was "loosened," again, just as had happened with the baboons.[13] Dr. Gordon, who was also the medical director of a film company, then showed a film of him carrying out this study. One subject was a middle-aged, anesthetized woman. "That's my wife," I remember Dr. Gordon saying. "The others wouldn't volunteer for it unless I did the experiment on her first."

What Dr. Gordon failed to offer, however, were reasonable answers to numerous questions his studies raised. For example, were the results pertinent, given that the meat was merely loosened and not expelled? Can one look into a baboon's throat—or anyone's throat, for that matter—and detect that a piece of meat has indeed been loosened? Since anesthesia relaxes throat muscles, would the administration of anesthesia more likely explain what caused the meat to loosen?

Red Cross officials then got into a discussion to determine just how many back slaps a rescuer should deliver to save a choking victim. Based on what I recall from the ensuing discussion, the number seemed quite arbitrary.

"How about twelve?" someone said.

"No; they would be dead by that time," another official objected.

"How about two?" someone else asked.

"No; that would look like we're not doing anything," responded another advisor.

The officials settled on four.

Equally strange was what the researchers of the 1976 *JACEP* airflow study concluded. Despite finding that back slaps had been "so ineffective in creating air flow or increased pressure within the chest," the study, whose author was anesthesiologist and Red Cross advisor Charles Wayne Guildner, still recommended that a rescuer first apply four "back blows" and, if ineffective, repeat the "abdominal or chest thrust . . . until effective or until victim becomes unconscious."[14]

Figure 14.1. *Battling against back blows*: I fought for years to try to get the American Red Cross to stop teaching people to hit a choking victim on the back.

RED CROSS TEACHINGS ARE EXPOSED

It is mindboggling that an organization set up to help the public good would insist on teaching a first-aid method with so little proof of its effectiveness. Organization officials have certainly been aware of the fact that saving a choking victim is a race against the clock. Death occurs four minutes after the onset of choking. A lack of oxygen for less than that time can cause brain damage. I believe that delaying the use of the maneuver by hitting people on the back hastens the possibility of death, paralysis, or a comatose state.

I have thoroughly researched the back-slap issue, and there is a plethora of evidence proving (1) back slaps cannot expel an object from a choking person's throat and (2) back slaps can lodge an object tighter in the throat of a choking person who initially is breathing, causing his or her airway to become completely blocked.

As an example, B. Raymond Fink, a University of Washington professor of research anesthesiology, proved at the 1976 National Academy of Sciences conference that, when a choking person is hit on the back, the obstructing object goes down deeper and tighter into the airway rather than loosening. Physiologically, the mechanics of this is intuitive and easy to visualize: back slaps cause the body, including the airway (larynx), to move forward. But the object, say, a piece of meat, does not move. Therefore, it ends up deeper in the airway, blocking breathing and causing death.[15]

The potential harm of the Red Cross recommending back slaps was exposed further in a syndicated article from the *Washington Post* that appeared on April 22, 1979. The story was written by Jean Carper, who, herself, had choked on food in a restaurant in Washington, DC. Ms. Carper described the incident, explaining that when patrons first saw what was happening, some hit her on the back, which failed to dislodge the food stuck in her windpipe. Then a waiter saved her life by applying the Heimlich Maneuver.

Ms. Carper's article, titled "Beware the Back Slap If You're Choking to Death," bluntly criticized the Red Cross for continuing to teach people to hit choking victims on the back. "The Red Cross has not adopted and does not teach the Heimlich technique, even though the maneuver has now saved thousands of people. . . . Instead, the Red Cross teaches a bastardized version of the maneuver which Dr. Heimlich charges is injuring and killing people instead of saving them."[16]

Ms. Carper explained that the Red Cross had failed to answer the elephant-in-the-room question: *Why continue to teach back slaps?*

"I have asked the Red Cross several times for evidence on the effectiveness of its method. Its response goes like this: The Red Cross is not a 'medical' organization; therefore, it relies on 'medical advice' from the National Academy of Sciences. An Academy committee in 1976 recommended the procedures the Red Cross teaches, including backslapping. The Red Cross has no obligation to dispute, confirm or investigate the validity of the recommendations." Carper noted that the head of the Red Cross's national first-aid program referred her to a report written by the National Academy of Sciences, but she found no evidence in the report that supported back slapping. Instead, she found twenty-five references, seventeen of which were unrelated to back slaps, while seven others provided evidence *against* back slaps. The one study that seemed to support back slaps was the one involving anesthetized baboons that Archer Gordon had discussed at the 1976 Red Cross meeting.

In 1982, a new and enlightening study, conducted by the Yale University School of Medicine and the John B. Pierce Foundation, was published in *Pediatrics* and seemed to put to rest the question of whether back slaps work or are harmful. In "Choking: The Heimlich Abdominal Thrust vs. Back Blows: An Approach to Measurement of Inertial and Aerodynamic Forces," researchers found that previous studies had failed to quantify the intense air pressure generated by the Heimlich Maneuver versus other thrusts, including back blows.

"Our data . . . show that the Heimlich maneuver is a powerful one," wrote the researchers. Furthermore, they proved what I had been saying for so long: because of the way back blows "cause an upward acceleration of the neck and upper back of more than three times the force of gravity," they wrote, it is "logical to imagine that in the case of partial obstruction, a back blow could transform the situation into one of complete blockage."[17]

ABANDONING BACK SLAPS

In July 1985, Red Cross officials seemed to be coming around. The organization, along with the American Heart Association, made a joint recommendation that people use only abdominal thrusts to save a choking victim. According to the organizations' press releases, they felt that both back blows and abdominal thrusts were effective but that the decision to drop back slaps was to simplify the teaching of first aid. Spokespeople for both groups stated that the adoption of the Heimlich Maneuver was still under review and that it was not expected to be officially adopted until the following year.[18]

During this time, I was urging US surgeon general C. Everett Koop to make a statement on the maneuver. Five years before, he had saved his young grandson from choking on a large chunk of meat. After applying the Heimlich Maneuver, Koop told reporters that the meat "shot about four feet across the room."[19]

A few months after the Red Cross and the American Heart Association announced that they were considering abandoning back slaps, Dr. Koop made a bold statement: "Millions of Americans have been taught to treat persons whose airways are obstructed by a foreign body by administering back blows, chest thrusts, and abdominal thrusts. Now they must be advised that these methods are hazardous, even lethal," Dr. Koop wrote. "The Heimlich Maneuver is safe, effective, and easily mastered by the average person." Furthermore, he wrote, "I urge the American Red Cross, the American Heart Association, and all those who teach first aid to teach only the Heimlich Maneuver. Manuals, posters, and other materials that recommend treating choking victims with slaps and chest thrusts should be withdrawn from circulation," wrote Dr. Koop.[20]

In 1986, the Red Cross and the American Heart Association formally released their standards and guidelines that endorsed abdominal thrusts as the only recommended response for choking adults and children victims.

At that point, I thought we were out of the woods. I was convinced that back slaps were a thing of the past.

I was wrong.

THE RETURN OF BACK SLAPS

In April 2006, twenty years after the Red Cross abandoned back slaps in favor of "abdominal thrusts," the organization brought back slaps back *as a first response to choking.* The move was done quietly. So quietly, in fact, I had no idea it had happened. But, indeed, the organization began teaching that rescuers aid a choking victim by administering a series of five "back blows" and then five abdominal thrusts.[21] The organization reaffirmed this position in 2010. (The American Heart Association continues to teach the Heimlich Maneuver—exclusively—for aiding choking victims.)[22]

Today, the Red Cross teaches rescuers to take this series of steps: First "send someone to call 9-1-1." Then "lean person forward and give 5 back blows with heel of your hand." After that, the Red Cross says one should "give 5 quick abdominal thrusts," and then "repeat until the object the person is choking on is forced out and [the] person breathes or coughs on his or her own."[23]

You don't have to peruse an empirical study to understand the danger of teaching people to use back blows to save someone who is choking. Simply consider the perspective of the victim: the frightening experience of having one's air supply cut off, the agony of being hit on the back to no avail, and, finally, the relief of regaining the ability to breathe after having been saved by a one, two, or three quick, upward thrusts to the diaphragm.

Joan Nathan, a renowned writer of Jewish cookbooks, described in a 2009 *New York Times* op-ed what this experience was like when she choked while at her home in Washington, DC. At the time, she was giving a dinner party for celebrity chefs.

"You would think that a house full of chefs would be the safest place if you were choking," wrote Ms. Nathan. "But, unfortunately, more people have heard of the Heimlich maneuver than actually know to administer it."

Ms. Nathan explained how she tried to swallow a large chunk of chicken. "For perhaps a minute, I stood there, praying that it would slide down my esophagus. Suddenly, it was stuck. I bent over to try to breathe." Two men saw her distress and slapped her on the back. It did nothing. Then another man stood behind her and asked if she could talk. Ms. Nathan shook her head.

"The next thing I knew he was placing his fists below my diaphragm and applying sudden, sharp pressure just below my rib cage to force the air out of my lungs in the Heimlich maneuver." After two tries, "the chicken popped out of my windpipe, leaving me with nothing but a slightly sore throat." (Her "knight in shining armor" was Tom Colicchio, a judge on the television show *Top Chef*.)[24]

It is common, when I introduce myself to people, for them to tell me that they have saved someone using the maneuver or that they, themselves, were saved. Studies continue to support the use of the maneuver.[25] Conversely, despite my repeated requests to the organization, the American Red Cross has never provided to me empirical evidence proving that back slaps can save the life of a choking person.

I have a Google alert set to "Heimlich Maneuver," so that I read about someone choking and being saved with the maneuver on a daily basis, often more frequently. Sometimes, those news reports describe a choking victim being hit on the back. When nothing happens, the individual is then saved with the maneuver. Other times, when the maneuver is not applied, the individual dies or suffers brain damage or both.

For example, on July 24, 2013, a news story emerged from Farnworth, England, about a woman who was having dinner with her boyfriend, Neil Whitcher, at a restaurant when she began to choke. Fifty-six-year-old Helen Marie Peploe did what many restaurant patrons do when they choke: they leave to avoid embarrassment. Ms. Peploe went into the restaurant's restroom; Mr. Whitcher quickly followed her. Later, he told the media that "she was suffocating," but he "couldn't get round her properly" to perform the Heimlich Maneuver, so he began "banging her on the back."

Mr. Whitcher said he was "terrified and panicking and shouting for her to keep fighting," but it was no use. Ms. Peploe collapsed and was then taken to the hospital, where she remained in a coma and then died. What is particularly shocking is how the article covering the story ends with instructions for how to save the life of a choking person. The newspaper's advice? "Give up to five sharp blows between the person's shoulder blades with the heel of your hand," and, if the blockage has not cleared, "give up to five abdominal thrusts."[26]

I believe nothing I could say could drive home the dangers of back slaps better than an e-mail I received from Innes Mitchell, a professor at St. Edwards University in Austin, Texas, on May 9, 2013. In 2010, Dr. Mitchell had brain surgery that resulted in his left vocal cord being paralyzed. Consequently, he has difficulty swallowing and is prone to choking when he eats. A few months after his operation, Dr. Mitchell and his sister were enjoying Sunday breakfast at a restaurant when he began to choke on his food. His sister began to thump him on the back.

"I could feel the force of her blows vibrate through my chest, but her efforts lodged the obstruction more firmly and tightly in my airway," Dr. Mitchell wrote. "I was in no position to tell her to stop, but I remember taking a few steps away. . . . I began experiencing the onset of oxygen deprivation, namely vision blurring and physical weakness." Another restaurant patron then rushed up and performed the Heimlich Maneuver on Dr. Mitchell. After four or five thrusts, the food dislodged and he was able to breathe again.

"It was an exhausting experience and I took several minutes to recover," he wrote, "but I have no doubt the man who performed the Heimlich Maneuver saved my life that Sunday morning." Dr. Mitchell thoughtfully suggested that when people hit a choking victim on the back, they could trigger a "bystander effect" in which potential rescuers hesitate to intervene because they assume that the choking victim is being helped. "This delay in performing the Heimlich Maneuver can waste critical seconds and turn an already critical situation into a deadly one," he wrote.

Dr. Mitchell has choked on food twice since that episode. Each time, his wife has performed the Heimlich Maneuver to save him. When he goes to a restaurant today, he looks for a poster depicting instructions for how to save a choking victim and is relieved when those instructions say to perform the Heimlich Maneuver.

I have no desire to diminish the good work that the American Red Cross has done, but by recommending back slaps, the Red Cross is putting people's lives at risk unnecessarily. I again call on the American Red Cross to stop promoting back slaps as a method to save the life of a choking victim and to adopt exclusively the Heimlich Maneuver as the preferred method. If the organization were to do that, I would gladly allow it to use the name *Heimlich Maneuver* in its teaching materials.

As Innes Mitchell wrote in his e-mail, "Choking is a dreadful and frightening experience. I believe the back slapping protocol advocated by the Red Cross is dangerous and could possibly jeopardize the safety of choking victims. Back slapping complicates an already traumatic situation and should not be disseminated as public knowledge by a reputable health organization."

Jean Carper stated as much in her article. "A reputable organization like the Red Cross that enjoys the public trust should not hide behind bureaucratic buck-passing when lives are at stake." Carper added, "In the meantime, if I'm ever choking again, I'd prefer my rescuer to forego the back slaps. Just the Heimlich maneuver, please."[27]

15

THE GIFT OF BREATH: THE HEIMLICH MICROTRACH

We often take for granted our ability to breathe. But for many people, like patients afflicted with such lung-related illnesses as emphysema, cystic fibrosis, severe asthma, pulmonary hypertension, and chronic obstructive pulmonary disease (COPD), breathing is a real struggle. Children with cystic fibrosis are also impacted.

I remember one day, during the 1980s, when I was visiting with patients at Deaconess Hospital. (By that time, I was a member of the surgical staff there.) I observed several patients receiving oxygen and noticed that they were tethered to oxygen tanks by a thin tube that delivered oxygen through a cannula, a small, plastic, two-pronged device that sits in the nose. To keep the cannula in place, the tubing ran on either side of the patient's face and over the ears. The patients looked exhausted as they strained to take in each breath.

Soon I would learn why patients taking oxygen strain to breathe, and I would come up with a simple device that would relieve the strain.

～～

Many Americans need to receive oxygen to live, as the number of patients who suffer from lung disease is staggering. Chronic obstructive pulmonary disease is the fourth leading cause of death in the United States, accounting for more than 120,000 deaths per year and costing more than $30 billion per year. It has been estimated that more than 24 million Americans have COPD.[1] Back in 2005, the National Lung Health Education Program estimated that approximately 1.2 million Americans were on long-term oxygen therapy.[2]

To breathe normally—or to try to breathe normally—these patients need special equipment. Fortunately, this equipment has improved in the last thirty years. Rather than be dependent on oxygen tanks, most patients use what is called an *oxygen concentrator*. A concentrator is the size of a small suitcase and provides oxygen therapy to patients at higher concentrations than are found in available ambient air. Unlike the old tanks that had to be filled with oxygen, concentrators plug in to an electrical socket and quietly generate oxygen from the air. Patients are usually connected to the concentrator by fifty feet of tubing. If they need to be any farther from the machine, which can weigh up to sixty pounds, they wheel it to the new location. To be even more mobile— say, if they want to leave their home—patients carry a small, five-pound tank of oxygen. The portable tank allows a patient about two hours of oxygen. To conserve the flow of oxygen so that patients get more breathing time, they can engage a "pulse flow" mechanism that emits a burst of oxygen only when the patient inhales rather than sending out a steady stream of oxygen.

But what hasn't changed since I took a look at those patients in the hospital many years ago is the way they breathe in the oxygen. Most still take in oxygen through the two-pronged, nasal cannula, which is still held in place by looping the oxygen tube from the cannula around the ears.

So what caused those patients I observed to be so exhausted carrying out the simple act of breathing? The problem lay in the delivery system—that is, taking oxygen through the nose.

THE STRUGGLE TO BREATHE

Why is taking oxygen through the nose so exhausting? Because it's wasteful. In fact, as much as 50 percent of generated oxygen does not end up reaching the lungs. The rest escapes from the nose and mouth. These escape routes make up something called "dead space." Patients are exhausted because they are trying to make up for the wasted oxygen—oxygen that should be entering the lungs but, instead, escapes.

There are other problems associated with taking oxygen nasally. The cannula can come out of the nostrils at night, interrupting oxygen flow. Also, it makes taking oxygen terribly conspicuous. Many patients would prefer others not be aware that they are taking oxygen, but the visible, pronged tubing in the nose, along with tubing encircling the head, makes hiding this act impossible. One woman told me how she felt humiliated when her grand-children visited her and asked, "Grandma, what's that in your nose? Are you dressed for Halloween?" Thereafter, whenever they were around, she chose to gasp for air rather than wear the embarrassing nose prongs. The "pulse flow" mechanism to conserve oxygen makes the problem of conspicuousness even worse. Each time the device pulses, it emits a clapping-like sound, which just about anyone nearby can hear.

Back in the 1980s, when I began studying the problems posed by the nasal cannula oxygen delivery system, I began to ask: Is there a more efficient way for patients to take in oxygen so that a lot more of it reaches the lungs? Was there a way to bypass the dead space or just avoid it altogether? If we could accomplish that, the patient could get more use out of a light, portable oxygen container. Today, I reason that such an improved system would reduce the need for the noisy, pulsing airflow-delivery mechanism as well as the large, cumbersome concentrators. And patients would not have to struggle so much to breathe.

A simple solution stared me in the face: Do away with the nasal cannula and, instead, deliver oxygen *directly into the trachea*.

A TINY, SIMPLE DEVICE

To allow patients to take in oxygen through the trachea, I needed to create a device that was lightweight, because the patient would have to wear it comfortably around the neck. The device needed to be small so it did not show easily. And it would have to be secure so that the oxygen flow would not be interrupted, even at night. After some study, I came up with a gadget that I believed would do the trick—something that I would call the Heimlich MicroTrach.

The MicroTrach consists of a three-and-a-half-inch-long, tiny, plastic tube, as narrow as a tube that is inserted into a vein for giving intravenous fluids. The tube is attached to a flat piece of butterfly-type wings made of soft plastic. The plastic wings rest against the neck, and a thin metal chain holds the device in place, strung through holes in the plastic wings. In 1991, I had the Heimlich MicroTrach patented.

The procedure for inserting the MicroTrach is simple. It's comfortable to use, and it can change people's lives forever.

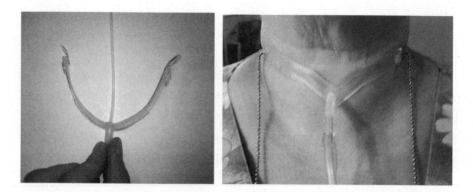

Figures 15.1. and 15.2. *A tiny device*: The Heimlich MicroTrach delivers oxygen through the trachea and into the lungs, eliminating the need for a nasal cannula. (Figure 15.2 *[right]* courtesy of Terri Lusane.)

The greatest advantage of the MicroTrach is that it allows patients to take in oxygen in a highly efficient manner. Unlike what occurs with conventional nasal tubes, patients breathe in nearly every liter of oxygen delivered, allowing them to make more use of a portable tank. What's more, because the oxygen enters the trachea below the dead space, the patient breathes quite normally.

Receiving oxygen through the trachea is safe. Animal studies done in 1974 proved that plastic transtracheal catheters were tolerated for more than a year with no irritation, mucosal lesions, or formation of mucus balls.[3] Another benefit of the MicroTrach is that insertion—performed by a medical professional—takes only about fifteen minutes. First, the patient lies down on his back with his head and shoulders resting on a small pillow; his head is bent slightly back, so that his neck is extended a bit. After injecting a local analgesic into the skin of the neck over the trachea, the doctor makes a tiny incision less than a quarter of an inch long. A long needle is pushed through the incision and into the trachea. Then a guide wire is inserted through the needle, into the trachea, and left in place as the needle is then removed. Next, the physician slides the MicroTrach tubing, with its winged plastic piece, over the guide wire and into the trachea, and the wire is removed. A jewelry chain is attached to the device and worn around the neck to keep the MicroTrach secure. The doctor then starts the flow of oxygen to the MicroTrach, turns off the oxygen that had been delivered through the nasal cannula, and removes the cannula from the patient's nose. The patient then returns once a month to have the device inspected, cleaned, and replaced as needed.

The idea of making an incision into the trachea might seem scary to some, but the hole in the front of the neck is hardly visible. In fact, it's only about the size of a hole in a pierced ear. Having such a tiny hole is not only much more cosmetically pleasing than the nasal cannula, it also reduces the possibility of infection. If the MicroTrach should come out accidentally, a doctor can easily reinsert it. The patient should not attempt to reinsert it, because a doctor can make sure that it is done under sterile conditions. Some patients may be advised to have on hand a backup oxygen-delivery system, which they can use until a doctor reinserts the MicroTrach.

A NEW LEASE ON LIFE

I performed the first insertion of a MicroTrach in July 1980 at Deaconess Hospital. The patient was a sixty-year-old man whom we'll call "Don." Don, who bought and sold engineering equipment, was stricken with emphysema and a chest injury. He had been confined to his home for seven years as he took oxygen through a nasal cannula.

Within a few minutes of inserting the MicroTrach into Don's trachea and starting the flow of oxygen to the device, he jumped up into a sitting position.

"What happened?" I remember him shouting. "I haven't breathed like this in years!"

Don had newfound energy after having been fitted with the MicroTrach. Four months after he received it, he required no further hospitalization for two years. When he did return to the hospital, it was for a condition unrelated to the MicroTrach device. Within a few months, Don was driving his car across the county for his job, and he continued to lead an active life until his death from pulmonary insufficiency five years after having received the MicroTrach.[4]

Other patients who received the MicroTrach also felt immeasurably better immediately after having it inserted. One of the most interesting cases was that of Thomas Stuber. I fitted Mr. Stuber with a MicroTrach in 1989. Mr. Stuber was so debilitated by a condition that prevented oxygen from moving to his bloodstream from his lungs that he had to be transported to Deaconess Hospital in Cincinnati by ambulance. He could not walk, and even sitting in a car for a short while was exhausting for him. Mr. Stuber's need for oxygen was so great that he breathed through a facemask that could deliver oxygen in large quantities.

Receiving the Heimlich MicroTrach changed Mr. Stuber's life. Within days, he was walking the halls of the hospital. After treatment, he not only walked out of the hospital, he also rode the several hundred miles home sitting in a car. Six months later, he was able to go to school and was much more physically active. His life only improved from there. Ten years after having received the MicroTrach, Mr. Stuber appeared in a cable television program called *The Real Me*, which chronicled my life. During the taping of the show, the audience watched a video about Mr. Stuber, who appeared to be in his midthirties at the time of filming. I was deeply moved watching him easily walk around, wearing his small shoulder bag containing an oxygen tank, chatting with friends, and putting on the golf course. During his interview, Mr. Stuber wore a pullover shirt that hid where the MicroTrach exited his trachea.[5]

"There is no question in my mind that, had the MicroTrach not come along when it did for me, I would not have been able to do things and probably most likely would have died," Mr. Stuber said in the video. Then he thanked me for inventing the MicroTrach. He said, "There has been no other thing that has helped me more in my ability to be active and to lead a much more normal life than I would have had otherwise."[6]

Many other patients who have received the MicroTrach have enjoyed similar experiences of rejuvenation. Before having it inserted, they were weak and fatigued, and their physical activities and social lives were extremely limited. Afterward, they had much more energy and lived normal lives.

"I call it the Heimlich Miracle," Nancy Horton said to a reporter in 1982 after she received the MicroTrach.[7] Ms. Horton, an advertising executive from Fairfield, Connecticut, who was stricken with emphysema was greatly debilitated by her disease and the cumbersome breathing equipment she had been using. But all that changed after receiving the MicroTrach.

"It's given me a whole new life," Ms. Horton told the media. "I'm now working at full capacity. I can do everything I did ten years ago and couldn't do one year ago."[8]

Another MicroTrach success story was reported in March 1990, when the *Shreveport Times* of Louisiana reported on an unusual wedding day.[9] Twenty-five-year-old John Stoddard had been sick with cystic fibrosis his whole life and could not leave the hospital. After I oversaw a physician insert a MicroTrach into Mr. Stoddard's trachea, Mr. Stoddard not only checked out of the hospital, he married his fiancée, Susan Gibbs. At the ceremony, an oxygen machine with a tube leading to his throat was hidden under his tuxedo.

"I thought I wasn't going to make it, but I made it all right," Stoddard told the newspaper. "A contagious smile was a fixture on his face," reported the *Shreveport Times*.[10]

Yet another patient who benefited from my invention was sixty-two-year-old Charles Robinson of Naples, Florida. Mr. Robinson was confined to a wheelchair and was suffering from a heart and lung condition that caused his health to swiftly deteriorate. As he relied on an oxygen tank with all the necessary tubes for his breathing, he felt his strength slowly draining away.

"I could never seem to get a deep breath," Robinson said in a media interview. "I was breathing shallowly as a matter of habit."[11]

But after receiving the MicroTrach, Robinson said he felt the improvement in his strength almost immediately. "I suddenly became aware I could take a really deep breath, like I had not taken in eleven years," he said.[12]

HIDDEN FROM VIEW AND CHEAPER

In addition to the ease with which they can breathe, patients who have received the MicroTrach have appreciated the fact that they get more breathing time with a portable tank, allowing them to be more mobile. Also, they can easily conceal the device with a turtleneck or a buttoned shirt. I once lectured on the MicroTrach at Yale University Medical Center, where I demonstrated the device for the media. Afterward, I said, "One person sitting here is taking oxygen through a MicroTrach right now." The reporters looked around the room, unable to detect who it was. Then, a patient from New Haven identified herself. She had been breathing normally with her small oxygen tank hidden in her purse.

Figure 15.3. *Easily hidden*: When patients wear clothing around the neck and store the oxygen tank in a shoulder bag, no one is aware he or she is taking oxygen with the Heimlich MicroTrach. (Photograph courtesy of Robert Horton.)

Dozens more patients benefited from the MicroTrach thanks to a study that was conducted by the University of Pennsylvania, both Beckley College and Beckley Hospital in Beckley, West Virginia, and the Massachusetts Department of Public Health in Boston involving forty-three individuals who were severely ill with COPD. Most were disabled miners who had black lung disease, emphysema, or both. Once a month, I came to Beckley, where I performed several MicroTrach insertions. The study followed the subjects from July 1981 through October 1982, after which time the device showed "significant improvement . . . for experimental patients and declines for the control group [who had not received the MicroTrach]." That is, patients who had received the MicroTrach experienced greater independence of daily activities, such as bathing, putting on socks and shoes, and rising from a chair. They showed improved ability to carry on normal activities without assistance, such as stair climbing, walking from house to car, eating at the dinner table, and completing meals without stopping due to shortness of breath. All the control-group patients, however, showed declines in those same activities. The study also showed that medical costs were reduced, as subjects who received the MicroTrach spent fewer days in the hospital than those in the control group.[13]

Interestingly, when the study concluded, I inserted a MicroTrach into the trachea of a man from Beckley who was a board member of the Benedum Foundation, which had funded the MicroTrach study. The man, who was in the advanced stages of lung disease, was so impressed with the results of the study that he wanted to receive a MicroTrach, too.

In 1982, I spoke at the annual meeting of the American Broncho-Esophagological Association meeting in Palm Beach, Florida, where I reported on fourteen patients who had been fitted with a MicroTrach. The group was comprised of male and female patients who were aged forty to seventy-seven years. Before receiving the device, all had been housebound and required wheelchairs to move around. After following the patients for two months to two years, I reported that thirteen of the patients were ambulatory and returned to many of their normal activities. What's more, patients' needs for oxygen were reduced by nearly 60 percent while maintaining normal arterial oxygen levels.

As was found in the Beckley study, medical costs were also reduced. Before receiving the MicroTrach, one patient's oxygen needs cost an average of over $400 per month; after receiving the MicroTrach, her average costs were only $145 per month. Furthermore, the patient previously had been hospitalized for nineteen weeks at a cost of $33,000 during the year before receiving the MicroTrach; during the first eighteen months after receiving the MicroTrach, she required no hospitalization for her pulmonary condition.[14]

My address to the association was reported in a July 9 article of the *Journal of the American Medical Association*. The journal commented that the MicroTrach "promises to free many patients with [COPD] from their reliance on cumbersome tanks, nasal cannula, and face masks."[15]

In the late 1980s, I conducted a more extensive study in which I inserted MicroTrachs in more than two hundred patients at Deaconess Hospital in Cincinnati and followed their progress over a six-year period. The study, which was written up in the medical journal *Chest*, showed the following benefits achieved by patients who received the MicroTrach compared to those who had been taking oxygen by way of nasal cannulas:

- no major complications or deaths
- virtually no oxygen waste
- patient compliance was superior due to no nasal irritation and improved appearance
- patients increased activity and resumed normal sleep habits
- returned sense of taste and smell and improved appetite
- required approximately half as much oxygen
- avoided accretion of large mucus balls
- decreased hospitalization and lung infections
- instillation of saline-solution cleaning method brought on coughing, which expels mucus[16]

Compared to conventional oxygen delivery systems, the MicroTrach—which costs $50–$150—requires less oxygen at less cost. And patients can rely on it for continuous, twenty-four-hour oxygen delivery because it has been found to remain in place at night.

THE NEED FOR PATIENT ACCESS

So, you may be asking, if this idea is so sound, why aren't people all over the world using it? Unfortunately, as most medical inventors know, coming up with an idea is only half of what it takes to get a product to market. Allowing patients to benefit from the MicroTrach means finding a company that will manufacture it. Over the years, a handful of companies have expressed interest and even begun manufacturing it, but ultimately they felt the selling price was too low for them to make a profit, so those companies gave up on the idea.

I'm pleased to say that, today, one manufacturer has expressed a strong interest in producing the MicroTrach and is looking at the cost to get it to market, so I have not given up hope that this device will finally be made available to the millions of patients who need it. In fact, I believe that the MicroTrach will become the technology of choice for most patients requiring oxygen. I know this because I have received letters from patients (and their loved ones) who have lived with lung disease and have been fitted with MicroTrach.

Martha Simmons of Aurora, Colorado, is one such correspondent. In 1981, I inserted a MicroTrach in her mother, who suffered from emphysema. Ms. Simmons wrote in a letter dated September 2, 2008, that her mother was a proud woman who often stayed at home because she did not want to endure the glances of others when she went out in public wearing her nasal oxygen apparatus. After the MicroTrach was in place, however, Ms. Simmons wrote that she was "somehow set free from her terminal medical condition." Ms. Simmons said her mother's stamina improved, and the opportunity to hide her medical condition from others did wonders for her self-esteem.

"I can honestly report that thanks to you and your transtracheal oxygen procedure, my mother experienced an additional five wonderful years of life with her family and friends," wrote her daughter. "Each of the Simmons family members is most grateful to you, Dr. Heimlich, for giving us five more years with our beloved mother. What a gift, the gift of life!"

Figure 15.4. *Keeping it simple*: The Heimlich MicroTrach and the Heimlich Chest Drain Valve are two devices that have improved and saved the lives of many and will continue to do so. (Photograph from Jan K. Herman, *Navy Medicine*.)

16

MAKING THE MOST OF GOOD IDEAS

I f I have a gift, it's an ability to see shortcomings in medical treatments—some that have been used for decades—and improve on them.

Throughout my career, I have been recognized with numerous awards for medical innovation. Such awards include the 1981 Distinguished Service Award, presented by the American Society of Abdominal Surgeons; the 1984 Albert Lasker Award; and the 1985 American Academy of Achievement Award. I was the guest of honor at the 1992 National Awards Dinner of the Maimonides Research Institute. In 1993, I gave the 1993 Chevalier Jackson Lecture for the American Broncho-Esophagological Association. I was inducted into the Engineering and Science Hall of Fame in 1984 and into the Safety and Health Hall of Fame International in 1993.

My devotion to saving lives has never ceased. From 1963 to 1968, I was president of Cancer Care, a national nonprofit organization headquartered in New York City that is part of the National Cancer Foundation. While I headed the organization, we worked with congressional lawmakers toward the passage of a bill that was signed into law by President Lyndon B. Johnson on October 6, 1965. The law established centers for research and treatment of heart disease, cancer, stroke, and other diseases. It was an unforgettable honor to have President Johnson personally hand me a pen that he had used it to sign the measure into law—a law that helped many patients with serious diseases find treatment at specialized facilities.

Christian theologian and author Norman Vincent Peale once declared that I had "saved the lives of more human beings than any other person living today."[1]

Figure 16.1. *A presidential gift*: On October 6, 1965, President Lyndon B. Johnson gave me the pen he used to sign into law a bill I had helped bring about, a law that would establish treatment centers for patients with serious diseases, such as cancer and stroke.

Some of my ideas have been adopted the world over, while some have not been fully put to the test. And I'll be the first to admit that a number are controversial and, in some ways, unorthodox.

Sometimes, though, my ideas consist of studying methods that are already known and applying them in new ways. Just as I used the oral antibiotic sulfadiazine to topically treat eye infections during World War II, I have taken other good ideas and put them to use in ways that others haven't tried, whether those ideas were invented by me or other researchers. Either way, this kind of "recycled medicine" can be just as effective at saving lives as coming up with a whole new approach. Some examples include using the Heimlich Maneuver to help victims of drowning and those suffering from asthma, teaching stroke victims and other patient how to swallow again, and treating HIV and AIDS with malariotherapy.

USING THE HEIMLICH MANEUVER FOR DROWNING

When I first came up with the Heimlich Maneuver, I hadn't considered that it could be used to save drowning victims. The first time I took notice of this possibility was when I read a story in the *Chicago Daily News* that appeared on August 24, 1974, two months after the maneuver was introduced.[2]

Dr. Victor Esch, the chief surgeon for the Washington, DC, fire department and an advisor on water safety for the American Red Cross, was vacationing on Delaware Bay when a lifeguard brought an unconscious drowning victim onshore. Dr. Esch applied the maneuver on the seemingly lifeless man. "I used the Heimlich technique that I had read about in the paper," Dr. Esch told the *Daily News*. "The water gushed out of his mouth and he began breathing. He had to be treated for pneumonia, which proved he had water in the lungs." The man was treated in the hospital for two days and later released.[3]

The number of people who drown in the United States each year is alarming: Nearly 3,800 drowning deaths occurred in 2010, the latest year in which statistics are available.[4] In 2009, drowning was the leading cause of accidental death in children from ages one to four years.[5] More than half of all drowning victims in the United States require hospitalization or need to be transferred to some other facility for care. Drowning victims can suffer brain damage that may result in long-term disability, including memory problems, learning disabilities, and permanent loss of basic functioning.[6]

To treat a drowning victim, the American Red Cross and the American Heart Association recommend calling emergency services and performing cardio-pulmonary resuscitation (CPR).[7] CPR is a method that uses a combination of breathing into the mouth and chest compressions to try to restore circulation and breathing to a person who is not breathing or has no pulse. Unfortunately, CPR, when used in drowning cases, has had only moderate success.[8]

I agree with Dr. Esch that the Heimlich Maneuver could be useful in saving drowning victims. To understand why, it's first important to take a look at what happens when someone drowns. After a victim is no longer able to hold his or her breath, he or she is likely to aspirate and swallow water. For a short time, a conscious or unconscious person will experience laryngospasm, a constriction of the larynx that prevents water from entering the lungs. However, following this stage, laryngospasm relaxes, at which time water can enter the lungs.[9]

At least two studies show that the lungs of drowning victims take in water. In 1986, a study published in the *Journal of the American Medical Association* concluded that victims experience a "flooding of the lungs."[10] Another study, conducted in 1993 and published in the *New England Journal of Medicine* showed that approximately 90 percent of drowning victims "aspirate fluid."[11]

There is debate as to just how much water or fluid enters the lungs of drowning victims, however, I believe that the Heimlich Maneuver should be used to remove whatever fluid exists, after which CPR can be applied. My idea is that rescuers should get the water out, at which point CPR would be most effective. Rescuers trying to revive a drowning victim have very little time to act. If a drowning victim is unconscious and has water in the lungs, administering CPR rather than the Heimlich Maneuver as a first response can waste valuable time.

Is this idea controversial? Absolutely. But a number of people who have used the maneuver to treat a drowning victim agree.

Using the Heimlich Maneuver as a first response for drowning victims "may open up a new vista of resuscitation," Dr. Victor Esch told the media after he had saved the life of the drowning victim in Delaware Bay in 1974. "It does no good to do standard mouth-to-mouth breathing if there is water in the lungs or debris in the trachea from vomiting. The air won't get through."[12]

Using the Heimlich Maneuver to treat drowning victims is worth examining, especially when you consider how it has worked, according to individual reports. One example occurred in 1986 in Destin, Florida. Four-year-old Shawn Alexander and his friend, five-year-old Michael Odom, were jumping off a public boat dock into the bayou below. The fun turned to fear when Shawn's feet stuck in the muddy bottom, trapping him under the water.

Young Michael pulled the boy out of the water, but by the time he got Shawn to safety, he was unconscious. A bystander gave Shawn mouth-to-mouth resuscitation, but the boy did not respond.

At that time, Terry Watkins, Destin's fire chief and an emergency medical technician, was pulling his fishing boat ashore when he saw the man trying to revive Shawn. Chief Watkins had recently read an article about the Heimlich Maneuver used for drowning victims and performed it three times on Shawn. Each time, a cupful of water was ejected from the boy's lungs. After the third attempt, Shawn coughed up white foam and started to cry. He was taken to the hospital and released the next day in good health.[13]

When I learned about this case, I was struck by the bravery exhibited by both Chief Watkins and Michael Odom. So, in 1989, I presented each of them with a Save-A-Life Award on the television show *Rescue 911*, hosted by actor William Shatner.

Today, Mr. Watkins is a sixty-nine-year-old retiree but still works both as an EMT and part-time in the local sheriff's office. "I'm an advocate for the Heimlich Maneuver for drowning," he said, when contacted at his home in Destin on July 18, 2013. "I saw it work."

Another incident took place on August 13, 1995, in Jacksonville, Florida. Several police officers and Ron Watson, vice president of the US Lifesaving Association (USLA), raced to save two-year-old Deshun Richardson, who was drowning in the lake at Hanna Park. By the time Mr. Watson got to Deshun, he was lying lifeless on the lake bank, not breathing and without a pulse. The team first tried CPR, which yielded no immediate results.

"Nothing was happening," said Mr. Watson, who was contacted at his home in Harrison County, West Virginia, on July 15, 2013. At the age of sixty-eight, he is president of the Harrison County Commission in West Virginia, and he is still a USLA advisor.

Mr. Watson remembered that, before the incident involving Deshun, he had met me at a convention in Washington, where I was talking to audiences about the Heimlich Maneuver. When Ron and I spoke, I had told him that it was necessary to get the water out of the lungs of drowning victims before air could come in.

"So I did an upward thrust," said Mr. Watson, recalling his rescue of

Deshun, "and water gushed out of the boy's mouth. He started gasping for air. We did CPR again, then more 'Heimlichs.' The boy began to breathe again." Deshun stayed overnight in the hospital and was released the next day.

One aquatics-safety organization has researched various rescue methods for drowning and trains its lifeguards to use the Heimlich Maneuver (called "abdominal thrusts") while the victim is still in the water. The National Aquatic Safety Company (NASCO) was founded in 1974 and is based in Dickenson, Texas. NASCO stresses the need for rescuers to act quickly when a person is found unconscious in the water. It tells its lifeguards to administer five abdominal thrusts while the victim is in the water and is being moved to an extrication point. Once the victim is out of the water, NASCO trains lifeguards to administer CPR.[14]

According to NASCO's website, it believes in administering the abdominal thrust because it works well, does not do additional harm to the victim, delays the initiation of CPR for a very short time, and initiates "a respiration step early in the rescue sequence." NASCO adds, "The time between when a victim is in the water and non-breathing and when they are placed on the deck and conventional CPR is initiated is typically between two and four minutes. The step of this sequence that often takes the longest is the extrication from the water."[15]

The NASCO lifeguard manual states that performing the abdominal thrusts takes only four to six seconds. "There is strong evidence that abdominal thrusts can help in the process of ventilating a drowning victim who has experienced a loss of spontaneous ventilation," reads the manual.[16]

NASCO has documented cases in which abdominal thrusts were successful. The organization states that from 1999 to 2009, of the millions of swimmers who were guarded, twenty-eight lost respiration. Of those, fourteen were revived by using only abdominal thrusts; eight required rescue breathing after the abdominal thrusts; and two required CPR after receiving rescue breaths and abdominal thrusts. Four of the victims did not survive, however, "other factors precluded the abdominal thrusts from being a significant factor," according to a NASCO press release.[17]

The main criticism against using the maneuver as a first response to revive drowning victims is that vomitus, or regurgitation matter, could be inhaled.

It is true that drowning victims sometimes vomit.[18] However, the worry that the maneuver would lead to aspiration of vomit has not been proven. In fact, the claim is based on only a single case from 1987,[19] and in that case, the maneuver was applied much too late. NASCO points out in its press release that many people receiving artificial respiration or CPR will vomit while those procedures are being performed. Fortunately, NASCO lifeguards perform the maneuver as soon as they get to the victims while they are still in the water. "Our lifeguards are trained to position the drowning victim to reduce the chance of vomit being aspirated," says the NASCO press release.[20]

Too many adults and children drown every year in the United States. I believe that a large number of these deaths occur because rescuers are failing to remove water from the lungs because they are not using the Heimlich Maneuver before applying CPR.

USING THE HEIMLICH MANEUVER FOR ASTHMA

Twenty-five million people in the United States suffer from asthma. That's about one in twelve people, and the numbers grow each year, especially among African-American children. Many individuals try to prevent attacks by avoiding contact with asthma triggers, such as allergens. Patients treat asthma attacks by using prescription medicines, such as inhaled corticosteroids. Long-acting beta-agonists, also known as "blockbuster" drugs, treat airway constriction but have been linked to serious side effects, including death.[21]

The Heimlich Maneuver should be researched as a possible, natural, viable treatment for asthma.

As in my research into using the Heimlich Maneuver for drowning, I began looking at it as a treatment for asthma after people contacted me and let me know they had used it on people who were having asthma attacks. What's more, after the maneuver was applied, the asthma sufferer began breathing normally.

For example, in the early 1990s, I gave a talk at the International Platform Association in Washington, DC. After I finished my speech, I recall a woman raising her hand. "My sister is an asthmatic," she said. "One day when I was visiting her, she suddenly had an attack. She couldn't breathe and was turning blue. I was sure she would die. The only emergency measure I knew was the Heimlich Maneuver, so I did it. She immediately took a deep breath and recovered."

On November 15, 1995, I received a letter from a man from Utah whom I had met at a training program in Salt Lake City. He wrote that his four-year-old granddaughter had asthma, and the child's mother thought that the maneuver might be of help in the event of another attack. One night, the child had the worst asthmatic attack of her young life. Her mother performed the maneuver and, within a minute, the girl was breathing normally again. About four hours later, the girl experienced another episode and, again, her mother gave her the maneuver and the child's breathing returned to normal.

Three years later, I received a letter from the girl's mother, Stephanie Hagen. She wrote that she had continued to use the Heimlich Maneuver on her daughter because it had worked so well to curb her asthma attacks. She said she used "mini-Heimlichs" as part of the family's regular routine, and it helped with her child's breathing long before it reached the "panicked stage." Ms. Hagen noted that her daughter was receptive to the procedure, even asking, "Mommy, can you help me breathe?" when she felt an attack coming on. "She has probably had the healthiest winter in her life this year," noted Ms. Hagen, who added that her daughter still used asthma medication after receiving the maneuver, and they believed it helped the medication "work more effectively."[22]

I received a letter from Ms. Hagen dated January 19, 2009, when her daughter was eighteen years old. Her mother informed me that her daughter had grown out of her asthma when she was in her early teens. When contacted in the summer of 2013, Ms. Hagen reiterated that the maneuver had been very helpful at curbing her daughter's asthma. "When I heard years later that it was controversial, it made me sad because the Heimlich Maneuver had been so helpful to us. Doing the Heimlich Maneuver took away her fear a little. It would force the air out, she would gasp, and we would count until she could settle down and breathe again. It made us very happy."

After receiving numerous reports of this kind, I began to investigate the physiological basis for the Heimlich Maneuver as a lifesaving technique when used for an asthma attack. By looking at what happens when someone is suffering an asthma attack, it's quite easy to see how the maneuver could help.

Asthma attacks occur when muscles surrounding the airway contract. This narrows the smaller air passages, the linings of which are chronically swollen and inflamed, as is common in many asthma sufferers. Mucus that fills the airway acts as a valve; that is, when the asthmatic person breathes in, the airway opens slowly and air slides around mucous globs in the small air pockets, called *alveoli*, of the lungs. On exhaling, those mucous globs, known as *plugs*, clog the narrowed airways and act like a closed valve, so air cannot escape. Trapped air distends the lungs, making both inhalation and exhalation difficult or impossible. If this condition goes untreated for too long, the asthmatic cannot even inhale medication and can die.

Remember that the Heimlich Maneuver pushes up on the diaphragm, compressing the lungs and expelling air left in the lungs. When the maneuver is applied, it has the potential to provide airflow that can carry away mucous plugs, thus clearing the airway. The maneuver also evacuates the thin layer of fluid that coats the lungs, called *alveolar fluid*, allowing asthmatics to breathe more easily. This evacuation of mucus and alveolar fluid allows airflow in and out of the lungs, ending the asthma attack. When performed on asthmatics, the maneuver need only be done gently and smoothly because you are expelling air and mucus, not a solid object.

A 2005 study published in the *West Indian Medical Journal* provides evidence that the Heimlich Maneuver is effective for treating asthma. From August 2002 to July 2003, sixty-seven asthmatics aged six to sixteen years old were studied in Barbados regarding the efficacy of using the Heimlich Maneuver to treat asthma. Thirty-three patients received three Heimlich Maneuvers once a week whether or not they were having an asthma attack. Thirty-four acted as controls, and a researcher's hands were merely placed on each these patients' upper abdomen one day a week—no force was applied. For the entire group, respiratory-function tests were carried out at regular intervals, as were exercise-tolerance determinations and quality-of-life assessment. The tests showed "progressive improvement" in the study group compared to the control group, and no adverse effects were reported.[23]

Because of the way the maneuver assists asthma sufferers, it makes sense that it can be used in other situations in which people are having breathing problems. In an episode on the PBS television program *NOVA*, titled "Everest: The Death Zone," mountain climber David Carter was determined to reach the summit of Mount Everest in 1996. He suffered from chest congestion for a day or so prior to the summit attempt, but he felt the problem wasn't severe enough to nix the planned attempt. The group reached the 29,000-foot summit, but on the way down, Carter's breathing got worse. Fellow teammate Ed Viesturs called down the mountain for medical help. A medical expert in wilderness medicine on duty at the medical post below recommended the Heimlich Maneuver. Viesturs performed the maneuver on Carter multiple times, and Carter eventually breathed more easily and was able to continue down the mountain.[24]

One of the most memorable moments of my life was calling in to an Indiana radio show featuring Carter after the mountain-climbing event. The first words Carter said to me were, "You saved my life."

Asthma patients should first consult their doctors well before trying the Heimlich Maneuver as a remedy. Still, based on what patients have told me, the technique holds a lot of promise. It is in our best interests to continue researching the possible effectiveness of the Heimlich Maneuver to treat asthma, especially when it occurs in children.

TEACHING PATIENTS HOW TO SWALLOW

I am forever grateful for the time I spent with Mohammed Ben Driss Hayani-Mechkouri, the teenage boy who came from Morocco to undergo the reversed gastric tube operation. Never will I forget him taking a lick of ice cream that smoothly traveled down his throat and through his newly made esophagus.

But this could not have happened had I not first taught Hayani how to swallow—or, rather, how to relearn swallowing. Since he had gone so many years without swallowing, he had forgotten how to perform this simple act. The method I used, which I learned from a nurse who taught premature infants how to swallow, involved sucking Hayani's finger so that he could know what successful swallowing felt like. Then he sucked his own finger, trying to produce that same feeling until he was able to master it.

After using the technique with Hayani, I came across other patients who also suffered from disabilities that prevented them from being able to swallow. Take, for example, Orville Reiser, a forty-five-year-old teacher from Ohio who came to see me in 1972. In 1943, when Mr. Reiser was sixteen years old, he contracted bulbar polio, which left him with respiratory paralysis. When he was stricken with the disease, his throat closed and he was unable to swallow, so doctors passed a tube down through his nose and into his esophagus. Using an acepto syringe, the hospital staff fed him liquid food through the tube. During this time, Mr. Reiser was unable to swallow. He used handkerchiefs to catch his saliva. After six weeks, the tube was removed, and Mr. Reiser learned how to use a tube to feed himself. Three times a day, he passed the tube through his nose and down his esophagus, through which he passed warmed liquid meals consisting of different combinations of strained oatmeal, eggs, corn syrup, baby food, and milk.

Understandably, having to eat this way greatly impacted Mr. Reiser's life. "At sixteen years old, I had the world in a jug and a cork in my hand, and it kind of jerked the rug out from under me," he said when contacted at his home outside Portsmouth, Ohio, on November 10, 2013. But he finished high school and went to college at Ohio University. There, the dean permitted him to fix his meals in his room. For twenty-nine years, Mr. Reiser continued to feed himself using the tube. Then a man he knew saw an article about my work with Hayani and suggested he contact me.

By that point, Mr. Reiser had all but given up on finding a treatment for his swallowing problems. Doctors had told him that he would never swallow again due to his paralyzed pharynx. When he came to see me, we measured the length of his esophagus by putting a tube down his throat. I was able to determine that not only did the muscles in his mouth work fine, but his esophageal muscles were also functioning, although erratically. To investigate further, I decided to do what no other doctor had done: I would operate on Mr. Reiser to understand just what was preventing him from swallowing.

On March 23, 1972, I made an incision in the neck, exposing his upper esophagus. It was immediately obvious what had been causing the difficulty. A two-inch length of the esophageal wall was scarred and thickened, apparently due to irritation caused by the tube that had been initially left in his esophagus for six weeks. I set about removing the scar tissue. It was a delicate operation because I had to remove the scar tissue without perforating the lining of the esophagus. Once the scar tissue was gone, the walls of the esophagus could expand to at least normal size. Pleased, I announced to the operating room staff, "I could drive a truck through there!" In an operation that took less than twenty-nine minutes, the cause of Mr. Reiser's inability to swallow food for twenty-nine years seemed to have been corrected.

But Mr. Reiser's problems were not over. A few days later, he was still unable to swallow fluids and soft foods. He would start choking, and the food would spill upward out of his mouth. I passed a tube through his mouth and throat and then down into his esophagus. There was no blockage. As I continued to be troubled by Mr. Reiser's inability to swallow, I remembered my work with Hayani. I realized that, in all likelihood, Mr. Reiser, like Hayani, had also forgotten how to swallow. And so I decided I would try with him the same finger-sucking exercises I had done with Hayani.

Mr. Reiser and I performed the finger-sucking exercises several times a day. After a couple of weeks of this therapy, Mr. Reiser returned home, where he continued to use his tube to feed himself but conducted exercises to train his esophagus to swallow. It took a great deal of patience. Five or six times a day, he stood in front of the mirror and put a four-inch-long tube the width of his finger down his throat and tried to swallow. By that time, he knew how to emulate the sucking action needed for swallowing from the finger-sucking exercises we had done in the hospital. Then he would try to sip milk with soda. Each time, he spit up the liquid, but he could get it down a little farther.

Then, one night, the sip went down into his stomach. He rushed in and told his wife that he had swallowed. But when he tried to demonstrate this feat, he spit up the liquid. However, the next morning, he was again able to keep a sip down. That afternoon, he ate some gelatin. It was painstaking work that took twenty minutes to complete. "I broke out in a sweat, I was working that hard at it," Mr. Reiser recalled. After he had been home for a few weeks, he came to see me for a follow-up appointment. He had forgotten to bring his paper handkerchiefs for the one-hundred-mile trip to Cincinnati, but it didn't matter. "I swallowed saliva the whole way," remembered Mr. Reiser. During that visit, I was thrilled that he could swallow a small bit of water. We both were jokesters who were close in age.

When he sputtered the second sip, I said, "See what happens when you show off?"

Mr. Reiser's swallowing continued to progress nicely. A few months later, he was eating perfectly normally. Today, at eighty-seven years, Mr. Reiser appreciates no longer being tethered to a tube to perform the simple act of eating. While he maintains a sense of humor about it all—referring to himself as a "Gerber baby for thirty years"—he also recognizes how reliant he was on his equipment. "It's humbling to know I could have starved to death in a grocery store if I didn't have the tube with me," he said. When asked about her feelings regarding Mr. Reiser's ability to eat again normally, his wife, Donna, expressed how nice it was for the two of them to go to a restaurant and eat together. Before learning how to swallow, he would have fed himself before leaving home and then just sat with her while she ate.

I worked with other patients whose esophagi had been damaged in the same way, and they, too, relearned how to swallow. With this consistency of success, I presented my findings at the American Broncho-Esophagological Association conference in San Francisco in 1979, and the results were published in a major medical journal three years later.[25]

The finger-sucking method was now known to the medical profession as a way to help more than just premature infants. But I was to learn that it could help even more patients—namely, those who had lost their ability to swallow due to stroke.

After a stroke, loss of the ability to swallow results from permanent paralysis of muscles in the mouth and throat. This differs from what patients like Hayani and Mr. Reiser, who both had no paralysis but had forgotten how to swallow, experienced. Paralysis from a stroke is unilateral; it affects only one side of the body. If the stroke hits the left side of the brain, the right side of the body is paralyzed; if it hits the right side of the brain, the left side of the body is paralyzed.

What do we do, I thought, when some muscles in an arm or a leg are paralyzed? The answer is obvious: we exercise the healthy muscles, strengthening them so they can compensate for the paralyzed muscles and duplicate their function. Since sucking is the first step to swallowing, could we exercise the healthy muscles on one side of the mouth and throat of stroke patients and strengthen those muscles to enable them to sufficiently carry out the act of sucking—despite paralysis of the muscles on the other side—using the finger-sucking method? If that could be accomplished, could we then work on teaching those patients how to swallow?

To find out, I began working with stroke patients at various hospitals. I taught them the finger-sucking method and discovered that they could regain the ability to suck by exercising the mouth and throat muscles that were not paralyzed. I can only imagine what it was like for hospital visitors, seeing older patients sitting in wheelchairs in the hallways, sucking their fingers—let alone seeing me suck their fingers.

Once the finger-sucking method helped these stroke victims regain their ability to suck, I had to teach them next how to swallow. So I conceived of a new procedure. To understand how it works, try this: Put your finger on your Adam's apple (or, for those with less prominent Adam's apples, such as females, place your finger in the middle of your neck, directly below your chin; you should feel the hard, ribbed trachea). Now hold your finger there while you swallow. You can feel your Adam's apple move upward, then downward. In the same way, I had patients put their finger on my neck so they could feel my Adam's apple while I swallowed. They felt the Adam's apple rise up and come back down. Then they would try it on their own: each would put a finger on his or her own throat and tried to get the Adam's apple to do the same thing. Repeated attempts to suck one's finger followed by attempts to swallow strengthened the non-paralyzed muscles on one side of the patients' throats. (As with any medical technique, patients should consult their doctors before trying out this method or the finger-sucking method.)

From 1979 to 1982, I successfully treated seven consecutive stroke patients, aged fifty-six to seventy-one, in this manner. When I first saw them, they had not swallowed fluids or solids for a range of from five months to thirty-nine years following their strokes. Each progressed to eating all foods from ten to sixteen days after starting the Adam's-apple exercises.[26]

TREATING HIV AND AIDS WITH MALARIOTHERAPY

I have long been fascinated with the potential of malariotherapy to cure disease. Malariotherapy involves inoculating patients with a curable form of malaria that induces fevers at a manageable temperature and last for about two weeks. After three weeks, the malaria is cured with antimalarial medication, such as quinine or chloroquine.

For decades beginning in the early 1900s, malariotherapy was used to cure neurosyphilis. Neurosyphilis is an infection of the brain or spinal cord caused by a bacterium. It usually occurs in people who have untreated syphilis. Symptoms of neurosyphilis include blindness, unsteady gait, and eventually paralysis, dementia, and megalomania. Patients' symptoms can worsen to the point that the brain is irreversibly damaged and the person may die.

Around the turn of the century, neurosyphilis was the scourge of Europe. Mental institutions were filled with people who were in the final stages of neurosyphilis. In 1922, Dr. Julius Wagner-Jauregg, an Austrian doctor, published a study showing that malariotherapy cured neurosyphilis. While Wagner-Jauregg is not a hero in all aspects—he was anti-Semitic and a Nazi supporter—his medical research was commendable. In fact, he received the Nobel Prize in physiology or medicine in 1927 for his work with malariotherapy and neurosyphilis.[27]

Other researchers picked up where Wagner-Jauregg left off. From 1931 to 1965, the US Public Health Service and Johns Hopkins Hospital laboratories provided malaria-infected blood to US hospitals to cure neurosyphilis, resulting in the curing of tens of thousands of patients. In fact, it was during these early years when I first learned about the efficacy of malariotherapy for neurosyphilis. I was in medical school at the time and observed patients being treated using this method. Years later, in 1984, a paper by the Harvard School of Public Health that was published in the *Journal of Parasitology* cited thirty-six references on malariotherapy for neurosyphilis and concluded that, while the literature reviewed on treating neurosyphilis patients is "scattered," it appeared that "one-third of those treated with malaria went into full remission of variable duration."[28]

Around the 1940s, penicillin became the standard cure for syphilis. This treatment prevented the disease from morphing into neurosyphilis. As neurosyphilis cases declined, so did the need for malariotherapy.

Still, just as malariotherapy cured neurosyphilis, I believe it has the potential to cure acquired immunodeficiency syndrome (AIDS).

People with AIDS have the human immunodeficiency virus (HIV). About fifty thousand Americans get infected with HIV each year (in 2010, there were around 47,500 new HIV infections in the United States).[29] About 1.1 million Americans were living with HIV at the end of 2009, the most recent year statistics were available.[30] In the United States, about 15,500 people with AIDS died in 2010.[31] Since 1981, 60 million people have contracted HIV, and 25 million have died of AIDS-related causes worldwide.[32]

AIDS is costly to treat and research. In 2010, the United Nations stated that its 2009 budget of nearly $16 billion aimed at halting the spread of AIDS was $10 billion short of what was needed for the following year.[33] In 2014, the US government will likely spend around $20 billion on AIDS alone.[34] To put that into perspective, the average AIDS patient in America takes a combination of drugs that add up to around $14,000 a year.[35]

Yet, despite the astounding loss of life and the huge costs, no one has yet been able to come up with a viable AIDS vaccine. It is time to seriously consider finding a cure for AIDS, and I believe that the answer could be malariotherapy.

Consider two studies that I coauthored. Both looked specifically at whether giving malaria to patients with HIV could improve their health. The studies, published in 1997 and 1999, were conducted in China.*

The first study followed two patients with HIV who were given malaria and then cured of that illness with antimalarial medication. Two years after the malaria was cured, the patients' CD4 counts rose "significantly" and remained at "normal levels" without further treatment "of any kind." (A CD4 count reflects white blood cells that fight infection. CD4-count tests determine how strong the immune system is and indicate the stage of a patient's HIV disease.) Furthermore, over the two years after being cured of malaria, "the patients remained clinically well." Another six HIV-positive patients were given malaria and were followed for six months, during which time they also "remained clinically well."[36]

The second study continued to monitor these eight HIV-positive patients over a two-year period. All eight patients "remained asymptomatic of HIV infection and felt stronger" after being cured of malaria. The study concluded that "malariotherapy basically is safe for HIV infection" in that the treatment seems to improve "some immunological parameters of HIV patients." For example, CD4 levels increased in five of the eight patients.[37]

Some skeptics have questioned whether it's a good idea to give someone with a compromised immune system another disease. Of course, I share the same concern. However, I believe that if the right strain of malaria is chosen and is administered carefully, the treatment is safe. I draw this conclusion partly from the success that malariotherapy has had when administered to patients with neurosyphilis, but I also find promise in a 1991 study conducted by the US Centers for Disease Control and Prevention (CDC) and published in the *New England Journal of Medicine*.

In the study, researchers followed for thirteen months 587 children who were in a hospital in Zaire. Some of the children were HIV positive, having been born to HIV-positive mothers, while others were not HIV positive. At the same time, some children in both groups had malaria. After monitoring the children, the study's authors concluded that "malaria was not more frequent or more severe" in children who were HIV positive than those who were not HIV positive. Furthermore, malaria "did not appear to accelerate the rate of progression of HIV-1 [the most common strain of HIV] disease."[38]

These three studies are significant because they show that malariotherapy can have a positive effect on HIV patients. What's more, giving malaria to patients with AIDS does not necessarily harm them. Given the positive effects that malaria has on patients with HIV, malariotherapy could be the answer to our finding a cure for AIDS.

Using earlier-known medical innovations in new ways to help victims of drowning, asthma sufferers, stroke patients, and those with HIV and AIDS has been an encouraging and rewarding aspect of my career. I realize some of these concepts don't sit well with some critics, but creative ideas are almost always attacked. Does such criticism bother me? Sometimes. But I don't think it should stop me from talking about ideas that I believe could help people.

The Athenian statesman Pericles wrote, "Having knowledge but lacking the power to express it clearly is no better than never having any ideas at all." For me, that statement reflects the story of my life. I feel the urge to teach my ideas to others so that those ideas can be safely put into practice or at least researched.

For many years, even my most widely used innovations have been criticized by my peers or simply dismissed. This kind of debate is healthy, but we also should not turn a blind eye to an approach just because it's never been tried before. The goal is to expand our limits and capabilities toward the goal of improving public health and saving lives. As a progressive society, we have a duty to scientifically evaluate medical claims and innovations before accepting or rejecting them.

That's what creative medicine is all about.

WORKING TOWARD A CARING WORLD

A t the time of this writing, I am ninety-three years old and still working hard to come up with ways to improve people's lives through medical innovation. I frequently get calls from journalists asking about my legacy. They want to know how I view my accomplishments. I often tell them that, when I look back over the more than seven decades of practicing medicine, I am inspired and humbled by the impact of my work. But my successes have also taught me about the importance of giving back to a world that has allowed me to touch people's lives in ways I never could have imagined.

This is especially true when I see how people have responded to learning the simple act known as the Heimlich Maneuver. For example, in June 2012, some forty thousand baseball fans joined me in a pregame ceremony to honor Cincinnati Reds third baseman Todd Frazier with a Save-A-Life Award. Mr. Frazier was being recognized for having used the maneuver to save the life of a man in a restaurant. When Mr. Frazier saw the restaurant patron choking, he did not hesitate. "I was the closest one, so I got over there," Mr. Frazier told the audience. "I gave two pumps, and it came out." When I got up to the microphone, I said that Frazier was amazing for having saved a life.[1]

While other innovations of mine have not received the same kind of attention that the Heimlich Maneuver has, I am filled with joy to learn that the Heimlich Chest Drain Valve has been used by military forces in a multitude of countries, sometimes on both sides of a bloody conflict. For example, in the 1960s, I introduced the Heimlich Chest Drain Valve to the Israeli army at a time when Israel was ensconced in wars in the Middle East. Then, in 1977, I visited Israel, and the Israeli authorities honored me for my contribution. My guides showed me several underground hospitals. Once inside, they opened an emergency medical kit, and the Heimlich Chest Drain Valve was sitting right on top. They took me to a military base in the Sinai Desert, where, again, the valve was readily available inside emergency medical kits. The valves were placed this way so that soldiers who needed to save a buddy had quick access to them.

As I stood in the middle of the desert, talking to these medical corpsmen and army doctors, I was mentally transported back to Camp Four in the middle of the Gobi Desert in 1945. I was vividly struck by the image of the Chinese soldier whose life expired before me due to a collapsed lung, a condition that could have been corrected by the Heimlich Chest Drain Valve. That dead soldier was the same age as my military guides. They wore similar khaki uniforms. I was so overwhelmed with emotion that I wept.

I remember another incident in which I was overcome with emotion. It occurred in February 1993, when I was invited to accompany a team of twenty cardiac and thoracic surgeons to Vietnam, a trip arranged by the citizen ambassadors of People to People International, an organization founded by President Dwight D. Eisenhower that brings together groups of Americans with their colleagues from other countries. In Hanoi, our plane was met by a contingent of North Vietnamese cardiac and thoracic surgeons. The head of the Vietnamese delegation introduced each member of our team until he came to me.

"Dr. Heimlich, you need no introduction," I remember him saying. "Everyone in Vietnam knows your name." I assumed he was talking about the Heimlich Maneuver, but, in fact, he was referring to the chest drain valve. "Your valve has saved tens of thousands of our people during the war, both civilian and military," he said. I never knew the North Vietnamese had used the valve during the war. It had been supplied to them by the Quaker organization American Friends Service Committee. The next morning, at a meeting of American and Vietnamese doctors, the chairman opened his session saying, "Dr. Heimlich will live forever in the hearts of the Vietnamese people." Hearing his words, I cried openly.

RETURNING TO CHINA

Thirty years after I had served as a navy doctor in Camp Four in Inner Mongolia during World War II, I returned to China. This first trip, which took place in 1984, and a subsequent visit in 1988 led me to fully appreciate what our medical crew had done for the Chinese soldiers and peasants when we treated their ailments for those eight months in 1945.

On the first trip, Jane and I had been invited to China by the daughter of General Fu Tso-Yi, the warlord who had ruled over the area where I was stationed and who had offered his soldiers to assist us in running the clinic. Fu's daughter, Fu-Dong, was famous for convincing her father to end the Chinese Civil War. At the age of twenty-two, Fu-Dong, who had been part of her father's inner circle, convinced him that the Chinese people had suffered enough with war and famine and that any more fighting would destroy the beautiful, historic city of Peiping (now Beijing). Fu sent his daughter outside the wall of the city, where she met Mao Zedong's forces and arranged a date when the gates of the city would be opened. As a result, Shanghai fell three months later and the war came to an end.

Fu-Dong, then a woman of about sixty years, arranged for Jane and me to be welcomed at a dinner in the Great Hall of the People (located in Tiananmen Square). Many officers of General Fu's army were present, and we had a jovial reunion. One officer remembered a basketball game between some Chinese soldiers and several of us Americans in which I, wearing clumsy army boots, fell head over heels to the ground. Others recalled the medical care I had given the patients at Camp Four.

On the second trip, I was invited back to China by one of General Fu's granddaughters, Xiou Dong. This time, I was taken to Camp Four. All of its buildings were gone and the road had been paved, but the waves of white sand stretching far into the distance were just as I remembered them. I tearfully knelt down and rubbed my hand in the dirt. As I stood up, our hosts motioned us to follow, and we walked across the road to a peasant's house on a small farm that I remembered from the war.

Figures 17.1 and 17.2. *Returning to a great country*: After World War II, I went back to China numerous times. I love the Chinese people.

Our conversation with the family who lived on the farm was a moving experience for me. The family members told me how they recalled the American soldiers riding their horses, waving to them, and shouting *"Hau bu hau!"* ("Good, no good?"), the Mandarin salutation for "How are you?" One woman told me that she remembered me treating her for trachoma when she was a child. I met others on that trip who told me I had treated them for trachoma, too. I wondered how many would have gone blind had I not come up with my sulfa-Barbasol treatment.

Two days later, I was driven to a small apartment house, where I was introduced to an elderly Chinese couple. My guides informed me that the man was blind. After some discussion, I was reminded that he was a doctor who had spent time with me in my clinic in 1945 and had given me a farewell banquet the night before I left the Gobi Desert. Being blind, he was having trouble remembering just who I was, since he had met not only me but also other doctors who had been at Camp Four before I served there.

I let him know that I was the only one who operated on people. A big smile erupted on his lips. He sat up straight and said through his interpreter, "You're the one who operated on the girl!" He remembered how I had saved the life of my first patient at Camp Four, the young woman who was brought to me on her father's back. The old man and I threw our arms around each other and hugged, both of us laughing.

SIGNS OF PEACE

As my parents taught me from a young age, we each have an obligation to give back, to help others in whatever way we can. For decades, I have been promoting the idea of what I call "A Caring World." It would be a program that promotes peace, good health, and goodwill worldwide. Through this program, people would learn what I have learned so well—that true happiness comes from the giving of oneself.

The first time I thought about the concept of A Caring World was in 1983, when I was giving a talk that was part of the lecture series at the Chautauqua Institution, outside Buffalo, New York.[2] Jonas Salk, inventor of the polio vaccine, was also on the program and talked about world peace. I spoke on the Heimlich Maneuver for saving choking and drowning victims, and I, too, concluded with my thoughts on world peace. I thought then that, while we each go on with our busy lives, it's important we never lose sight of the big picture—that is, to help bring peace to the world.

Many people today feel that the world is in a terrible state, and I can't blame them for feeling that way. We see photos of children holding guns or lying dead, and they look like our own kids. Yet I believe that it is more possible than ever to create a caring world. As we increase communication with the Internet, we bring people together in ways we could never have dreamed of when I was a young man. Choices we make here in America affect the environment everywhere else, and vice versa. Countries that used to hate each other are now interdependent; the need to work together toward goals that benefit us all is more apparent than ever.

History has shown us wonderful examples of this kind of give-and-take relationship in action. For instance, when World War II ended, US Secretary of State George Marshall established the Marshall Plan, the American initiative in which the United States gave economic support to help rebuild European economies to prevent the spread of Communism. The program enhanced the postwar economies of Germany and Japan, thereby enabling those countries to transform into world-friendly democracies.

In 1956, I passed through the Brandenburg Gate from West Berlin to Communist East Berlin, one city split in two by the Berlin Wall. On June 7, 1987, President Ronald Reagan stood at the gate and spoke of the industrial benefits of freedom, issuing his famous words, "Mr. Gorbachev, tear down this wall." Two years later, the Soviets did that very thing.

In the many years that I have been a surgeon, I have had the opportunity to work with some of the finest individuals in the field of medicine and have marveled at the care patients have received from nurses and aids. Some people with whom I have worked have ventured outside their normal fields for the sheer interest in improving the lives of patients. In the 1970s, I worked with astronaut Neil Armstrong on developing an artificial heart-lung system. I was impressed and energized by Neil's desire to help others when he could have chosen to simply rest on his laurels as the first man to walk on the moon. We remained friends until he passed away on August 25, 2012.

Figure 17.3. *A man who went beyond*: I appreciated astronaut Neil Armstrong's dedication to medical innovation. (Photograph courtesy of Kevin Grace.)

For about six years, Neil and I met for lunch on a weekly basis in my laboratory at the Jewish Hospital. He had obtained NASA's last two existing pumps that were used to circulate fluid in space suits to maintain a constant temperature. We worked on modifying those pumps to reduce the hemorrhaging of red blood cells during bypass surgery, a problem that medical pumps at the time were experiencing. We did not get to the point of developing a prototype; however, on March 20, 1975, we presented our findings at the annual meeting of the Association for the Advancement of Medical Instrumentation.[3]

Figure 17.4. *A devoted wife*: From the time that Jane and I were married in 1951, she was supportive of my work.

I believe I have learned the most about a caring world from my relationships with my children, my father, and my late wife, Jane. Jane devoted her life to caring for others not only as a wife, a mother, and a loyal friend, but also as a writer. As a columnist for the *Cincinnati Post* in the 1970s, she wrote an article about holistic health, which had not yet hit the mainstream. The article was so popular that Jane began to dig deeper into the subject. In 1980, she collaborated with a holistic-health physician to write a book on homeopathy called *Homeopathy at Home*, which was translated into seven languages. Then, in 1990, she wrote another book. *What Your Doctor Won't Tell You* explained alternative, holistic-health remedies in a way that was clear to the layperson. In this way, Jane's work helped thousands of patients who were looking for nontraditional healthcare treatments. After sixty-one wonderful years together, Jane passed away on November 10, 2012.

Figure 17.5. *Sixty-one wonderful years*: In our later years, Jane and I lived a relatively simple life. We enjoyed traveling to resorts in natural settings such as Wisconsin, North Carolina, and Maine.

Like their mother, our children are also compassionate, loving individuals. Even when they were younger, I could see how they cared about the wellbeing of others. In fact, back in the 1970s, when I was working with dogs in my laboratory to come up with the Heimlich Maneuver, my young daughter, Elisabeth, who adores animals, asked to come to the lab with me. From that point on, she held the dogs and walked them around the block whenever she had the chance. Both my son Philip and my daughter Janet are devoted parents. I admire the loving and mutually respectful relationships they have with their children, and I treasure the time I spend with my three grandchildren, Henry, Allie, and Maxine.

Figure 17.6. *Daughter and wife*: Me with my daughter Elisabeth and Jane in 1990. (Photograph courtesy of Elisabeth Heimlich.)

Figure 17.7. *At Jane's book signing*: My son Philip with his wife, Rebecca, and their children, Henry and Allie. (Photograph courtesy of Philip Heimlich.)

Figure 17.8. *Daughter and granddaughter:* My granddaughter Maxine and my daughter Jan. (Photograph courtesy of Janet Heimlich.)

A REWARDING RELATIONSHIP WITH MY FATHER

As a physician for more than seventy years, I have treated hundreds of elderly patients, but it was only in the last year and a half of my father's life that I truly learned about aging and how to care for those approaching death. That year, 1986, was the best year of my life. Here was a man I had known and loved longer than any other person, but we became true friends only during that last year together.

Pop had moved to Cincinnati, and he did his best to live independently, but eventually he needed our help. One evening, I answered the telephone and it was Dad. "Hank, I can't get up from the chair," he said. Jane and I jumped into the car and drove to his apartment. When I saw him, I realized he had not been eating enough and was too weak to stand. I debated whether to take him to the hospital or back to our house and decided on the latter. We bundled him in a blanket and drove home.

Pop's strength returned after he lived with us, and we were able to enjoy a wonderful year together. I began coming home after lunch and not returning to the office so I could spend more time with him. We had long talks after lunch and dinner. It was great to have a live-in male friend, and I began asking questions and saying things I had avoided for many years.

I remember one particularly wonderful moment.

"Dad," I said, "men of our generation are ashamed to say 'I love you,' but my kids taught me to say it. Pop, I love you."

"I love you, too," he responded warmly. We hugged and kissed as never before. Thereafter, on the phone or in person with visitors, with an expression of discovery in his voice, he closed every conversation saying, "You know what? I love you."

In his last six months, Pop's health worsened. His personal-care and medical-care needs required increasing time. Fortunately, a friend shared with me that, when she had had to spend time with her aging mother, she had been annoyed by the demands on her time and effort. Yet after her mother died, she missed performing those tasks.

Knowing this, I took pleasure in being able to spend more time caring for Pop. We sometimes had a role reversal. I would carry out the medical rituals, tuck him into bed, and give him a hug and a kiss. Sometimes I'd say, without being conscious of it, "Good night, my son." At other times, Pop would say he thought of me as his father.

Figure 17.9. *Taking in my father*: We loved having Pop visit throughout our lives. When he became aged, he lived with us until his death. (Photograph courtesy of Elisabeth Heimlich.)

A few months later, he told me of certain symptoms I, as a doctor, should have recognized as indicating urine retention. Sometimes when we care for loved ones every day, we don't see their small declines. When his condition became acute, I had his physician come over to the house. While waiting for the ambulance, Pop lay in his bed while I sat next to him with my arm around him. I knew we had reached a point of complete understanding when he said, matter-of-factly, "Hank, I don't want to live any longer. I'm just a burden now. I won't ask you to do anything because you're a doctor and it would be on your conscience." A few months earlier, I would have stammered through a denial of his impending death. Instead, I could say honestly, "I can accept your decision, Pop, and I won't prolong your life unnecessarily."

On admission to the hospital, he underwent a minor surgical procedure under general anesthesia, but at his age, it was still a major stressor. Fortunately, he recovered and was able to return home after about a week. Then, one day, he told me, "Hank, I don't know why I said I was ready to die. I really want to live." How wonderful to be ninety-nine years old, ill, and want to continue living!

On December 30, 1986, four months before his one hundredth birthday, Pop died at home. Up until the last week of his life, people were still phoning him for advice. He spent his entire life helping to create a caring world not only as a social worker but also as a humanitarian. His good deeds will remain forever in my heart and in the hearts of the families he touched.

ALLOWING CHILDREN TO BE SUPERHEROES

While reporters seem fixated on my past accomplishments, I am still quite active and continue to educate people about lifesaving programs. Today, I do so through the Heimlich Institute, a nonprofit organization that conducts medical research and teaches the public, including schoolchildren, how to save lives with the Heimlich Maneuver.

In some ways, I see teaching the maneuver as a way for people to connect to each other as thousands of people throughout the world learn to save the lives of friends, relatives, neighbors, and strangers. Recently, we at the Heimlich Institute got to bring that gift to the next generation by initiating a program we call Heimlich Heroes.

The idea came from Patrick Ward, who headed the Deaconess Associations Foundation (where the Heimlich Institute is housed) in Cincinnati. Pat and I had often spoken about how astonishing it is that young children learn the maneuver and use it to save a life.

One day, Pat suggested a tremendous idea: he proposed creating a curriculum for school children to teach them how to perform the Heimlich Maneuver. And that's just what we did. The foundation employed a gifted sixth-grade teacher with a doctorate in chemistry to develop the curriculum. Dr. Michelle Mellea teaches science at the Bethany School, a private Episcopal elementary and middle school in Glendale, Ohio.

To help instruct sixth graders about the maneuver, teachers use "Heidi Heimlich," a forty-two-inch doll specially created for hands-on training of the Heimlich Maneuver. The doll is designed and constructed to mimic human anatomy, complete with an internal diaphragm, lungs, a windpipe, and a plastic mouth that expels a peanut-sized foam cushion when the maneuver is demonstrated correctly.

On April 22, 2012, we rolled out a Heimlich Heroes pilot program involving Dr. Mellea's sixth-grade science class. The children loved the experience. They learned that they can save the life of a parent, a sibling, a friend, or even their teacher. It was delightful to watch the children master the technique of applying pressure to Heidi's diaphragm to compress her lungs, force air upward, and expel the peanut.

The children came away from the demonstration empowered and confident in their ability to react correctly in an actual choking crisis. Becoming a Heimlich Hero taught those kids not only a lifesaving skill but also self-esteem and a responsibility to help others in need. After the lessons were over, Bethany School's principal, Cheryl Pez, took me aside and told me a tragic story. She shared with me that her brother had died from choking in June of 2005 at the age of thirty-eight. He was at home, alone, when he began to choke on food. Not knowing how to self-administer the maneuver, he went to the house of a neighbor who was not home and collapsed and died in their driveway. For Ms. Pez, having Bethany School be the first to host the Heimlich Heroes program was a way to honor her brother's memory and spare another family the pain hers had suffered.

Since that first demonstration, the Heimlich Heroes program has really taken off. As of summer 2013, the program has been presented in ten

Cincinnati public and private schools; 523 sixth graders have been instructed on the correct way to perform the Heimlich Maneuver and save a life. We plan to expand the Heimlich Heroes curriculum to elementary-school systems nationwide. The program is priceless because it can help bring down the number of annual choking deaths in the United States today.

A CARING WORLD ON A GLOBAL SCALE

We must encourage caring throughout the world. A meaningful sense of values must be established and accepted by all countries and cultures. We should hold up caring individuals as role models for children and adults alike, and the media should publicize caring acts.

Governments can do their share, too. Just as anyone can perform the Heimlich Maneuver, governments can learn to care, to empathize, to give. Earlier, I discussed how we have seen huge changes take place in certain countries—changes that were unthinkable at one time, yet they happened and improved the lives of many.

For a long time, I have advocated for countries that have long been at odds with each other to start trading with one another and working together. Why? Because establishing such economic partnerships can lead to world peace.

The idea is simple: once countries form economic alliances, they prosper together. But the world can benefit from these alliances in ways we never imagined because countries can band together to reach out to less fortunate, developing countries to help them prosper, too.

As an example, in the spring of 1998, I was invited by doctors in Iran to lecture in their country. It was at the height of enmity between the United States and Iran. For two weeks, I gave talks at universities, hospitals, and a medical college. Before concluding my trip, I was invited to hold a press conference. One reporter asked, "What do you think of President Khatami?" I explained that I had seen a CNN interview with the president and agreed with his ideas about the United States and Iran working together. The newspaper *Iran News* covered the press conference with an article carrying the headline, "'A Caring World', the Slogan of Heimlich."[4]

But there is one key partnership that can get this movement going on a global scale—that is, the relationship between the United States and China. Having spent time in China during World War II and having visited that country numerous times since then, I have gotten to know many Chinese citizens and have found them to be wonderful people. It pains me that the United States and China have been at such odds for so long.

But how that has been changing! Now trade is expanding between the two countries, and the economies of both are benefiting as a result. In December 2012, US ambassador to China Gary F. Locke, who is of Chinese descent, spoke optimistically about the relationship between the United States and China. Mr. Locke pointed out that since the Nixon era, both countries have become inextricably tied to one another, and the relationship is bound to grow even more interdependent going forward. "Our economies are so intertwined, and Chinese leaders know that," Mr. Locke told the media.[5]

In my own city, the University of Cincinnati (UC) is partnering with a Chinese university in opening the International College of Medicine in Chongqing in Sichuan Province. The new school promises to create opportunities in research and clinical studies for both countries, since professors from UC and China will teach there. In addition, the school will allow students from both countries to study and come up with medical innovations together.[6] Most of the international students at UC come from China. According to Xuemao Wang, dean and university librarian of the University of Cincinnati Libraries, approximately 1,200 Chinese students were enrolled in 2013.[7]

With the economic and educational resources that both the United States and China will gain from these kinds of ventures, *both countries can partner to help the rest of the world.* Specifically, China and the United States can join together to help impoverished countries improve their economies and educational opportunities. In doing so, the countries receiving these resources would be less likely to engage in wars that plague this world.

If the United States and China were to see each other as partners in giving back together, *we will be on our way to being a caring world.*

I myself, have been on the receiving end of care throughout the world. In 1997, I collapsed at a public event. While I was being hospitalized, the hospital switchboard was overloaded for several days. Television and radio programs, as well as newspapers, carried the story. For months afterward, people came up to me and sent me letters, asking how I was feeling. I had no idea that so many cared about me as a person.

I have lived a long and wondrous life. I have seen the world as a son, a student, a soldier, a physician, a celebrity, and a humanitarian. I think back to my appearance on *The Tonight Show Starring Johnny Carson*: Was my trading jokes with Johnny and other publicized moments just entertainment? I think not. Yes, it gave many a chuckle, but I know that my celebrity status has helped others to learn about my medical innovations, giving them a power they might not have known they possessed—the power to save a life, perhaps their own life.

It's been estimated that I've indirectly saved hundreds of thousands of lives over the seventy years of my medical career. So, perhaps, that is my way of giving back.

When you save a life, you help save a world. And you know what? I'm not done yet.

MORE ABOUT HEIMLICH HEROES

Anyone can be a Heimlich Hero with his or her very own superpower: the power to save a life.

Approximately five thousand people choke to death in the United States each year, and the simplest first-aid action—proven to prevent a choking death—is the Heimlich Maneuver.

The Heimlich Heroes online training program can be used in a classroom, in an organization or a club, or in a group atmosphere. Your donation to the Heimlich Heroes program allows us teach the following to young people nationwide:

- recognize the signs of choking
- understand how to respond properly with the Heimlich Maneuver
- learn ways to help minimize the risk of choking

FOR MORE INFORMATION, PLEASE CONTACT:

Heimlich Heroes
330 Straight Street
Suite 330
Cincinnati, OH 45219

www.heimlichheroes.com
heimlichheroes@deaconess-cinti.com
(513) 559-2468

NOTES

CHAPTER 1. HEEEEERE'S HEIMLICH!

1. "Medical Student Wins Safety Council Award," *New York Times*, September 25, 1941.

CHAPTER 2. MY BEGINNINGS

1. Stefan Riedel, "Edward Jenner and the History of Smallpox and Vaccination," *Baylor University Medical Center Proceedings* 18, no. 1 (January 2005): 21–25, http://www.ncbi.nlm.nih.gov/pmc/articles/PMC1200696/ (accessed September 10, 2013).

CHAPTER 4. MEDICAL-SCHOOL CHALLENGES AND A STRANGE INTERNSHIP

1. "Hans Bethe—Biographical," Nobelprize.org, Nobel Foundation, http://www.nobelprize.org/nobel_prizes/physics/laureates/1967/bethe-bio.html (accessed October 16, 2013).

2. Chief of Naval Personnel Randall Jacobs to Lieutenant (jg) Henry J. Heimlich, navy orders memo, December 15, 1944, Heimlich family papers.

CHAPTER 5. EN ROUTE TO CHINA

1. Chief of Naval Personnel Randall Jacobs to Lieutenant (jg) Henry J. Heimlich and three others, navy orders memo, February 13, 1945, Heimlich family papers.

CHAPTER 6. A HEALTH CLINIC IN THE GOBI DESERT

1. The tenth man did, in fact, survive. "Berserk Sailor Kills Nine Men," *The Spokesman-Review* (Spokane, WA), April 23, 1946, p. 21.

2. "Sailor Killer Ends Own Life," *Lima (OH) News*, August 2, 1947, p. 10.

3. *Destination Gobi*, Twentieth Century Fox, directed by Robert Wise, released March 20, 1953.

CHAPTER 8. SAVING A LIFE AND FINDING LOVE

1. Jane Heimlich, *Out of Step* (Wilmington, OH: Orange Frazer Press, 2010), p. 63.

2. Ibid.

CHAPTER 9. RESTORING THE ABILITY TO SWALLOW: THE REVERSED GASTRIC TUBE OPERATION

1. Henry Heimlich, MD, and James Winfield, MD, "The Use of a Gastric Tube to Replace or By-Pass the Esophagus," *Surgery* 37, no. 4 (April 1955): 549–59.

2. Lawrence Galton, "Mrs. Dennis and the Miraculous Meal," *Cosmopolitan*, August 1960, p. 131.

3. "Along with Hot Controversies, Some Hot Medical Discoveries," *Life*, July 7, 1961.

4. "7 Operations Save Infant's Life," *TEMPO* no. 1 (Fall 1968): 7.

5. Henry J. Heimlich, MD, "Esophagoplasty with Reversed Gastric Tube: Review of Fifty-Three Cases," *American Journal of Surgery* 123, no. 1 (1972): 80–92.

CHAPTER 10. PERFORMING THE REVERSED GASTRIC TUBE OPERATION BEHIND THE IRON CURTAIN

1. James Winfield, MD, and Henry Heimlich, MD, "The Use of a Gastric Tube to Replace or By-Pass the Esophagus," *International Abstracts of Surgery* 101 (1955): 358–59.

2. Mary Tanenbaum, "County Surgeon Finds Reds Ailing," *Westchester News*, [date unknown].

3. "Amazing Surgery in Romania Described to Bergen Doctors," *Bergen Evening Record*, December 12, 1956.

4. Henry J. Heimlich, MD, "The Use of a Gastric Tube to Replace the Esophagus as Performed by Dr. Dan Gavriliu of Bucharest, Rumania; a Preliminary Report following a Visit to Bucharest, Rumania," *Surgery* 42, no. 4 (January 18, 1957): 693–95.

5. Henry J. Heimlich, MD, "Esophageal Replacement with a Reversed Gastric Tube," *Diseases of the Chest* 36, no. 5 (November 1959): 3.

6. "Dr. Heimlich in Film," *Rye (NY) Chronicle*, July 6, 1961.

CHAPTER 11. A PROMISE TO A DEAD SOLDIER KEPT: THE HEIMLICH CHEST DRAIN VALVE

1. Lieutenant Bradley to Dr. Henry Heimlich, January 24, 1966.

2. Ibid.

3. Gerald A. Baugh, MD, of the US Air Force, to Becton Dickinson and Company, April 11, 1966.

4. Ibid.

5. Edgar F. Berman, MD, personal physician to the vice president, to Mrs. Catherine H. Bradley, July 14, 1966.

6. "On the Scene Report: Medicine Battles the Odds in Vietnam," *Medical World News*, November 18, 1966, p. 112.

7. "News from the World of Medicine: Live-Saving Valve," *Reader's Digest*, September 1967.

8. Ed May, *BD Echo* (newsletter), December 2006.

9. Alyssa Jeff of Becton Dickinson, e-mail message to Karen Carmichael, June 5, 2013.

CHAPTER 12. A BOY NAMED HAYANI

1. "Arab Lad Is Pet at Jewish Hospital," *Medical World News*, March 19, 1971, p. 71.

2. Ibid.

3. Jane Heimlich, "Making a House Call in Morocco," *Cincinnati Post*, October 19, 1972, p. 61.

4. Ibid.

CHAPTER 13. SAVING THE LIVES OF CHOKING VICTIMS: THE HEIMLICH MANEUVER

1. For President Ronald Reagan and Nicole Kidman, see Lenore Skenazy, "Maneuvering over Heimlich," *New York Sun*, February 21, 2007, http://www.nysun.com/new-york/maneuvering-over-heimlich/48992/ (accessed November 3, 2013). For Elizabeth Taylor, see "An International Incident with a Happy Ending," *Barker* (official publication of Variety Clubs International) 14, no. 2 (November 1971): 15. For Goldie Hawn, see "Food Choking: The Heimlich Maneuver Isn't a Gag," Dr. John Hong, September 22, 2012, http://www.drjohnhong.com/blog/2012/food-choking-the-heimlich-maneuver-isn't-a-gag/ (accessed November 3, 2013). For Jack Lemmon, see Roger Ebert, "Walter Matthau: A Laugh-Filled Life," RogerEbert.com, July 2, 2000, http://www.rogerebert.com/interviews/walter-matthau-a-laugh-filled-life (accessed November 3, 2013). For Cher, see "Cher Describes Choking Incident," *Observer-Reporter* (Washington, PA), January 12, 1982, http://news.google.com/newspapers?nid=2519&dat=19820112&id=U6VdAAAAIBAJ&sjid=HF0NAAAAIBAJ&pg=1238,1391416 (accessed November 3, 2013). For Carrie Fisher, Ellen Barkin, Halle Berry, Dick Vitale, Ed Koch, and John Chancellor, see Stacy Conradt, "The Quick 10: 10 Celebrities almost Felled by Food," *Mental Floss*, September 29, 2008, http://mentalfloss.com/article/19718/quick-10-10-celebrities-almost-felled-food (accessed November 3, 2013). And for Joan Nathan, see Marisa McClellan, "Tom Colicchio Uses Heimlich Maneuver to Save Cookbook Author's Life," *Slashfood*, January 19, 2009, http://www.slashfood.com/2009/01/19/tom-colicchio-uses-heimlich-manuver-to-save-cookbook-authors-li/ (accessed November 3, 2013).

2. Henry J. Heimlich, MD, "Pop Goes the Café Coronary," *Emergency Medicine* 6, no. 6 (June 1974): 154–55.

3. Arthur Snider. "New Method Offered to Save Food-Chokers," *Chicago Daily News*, June 11, 1974, p. B1.

4. "News Article Helps Prevent a Choking Death," *Seattle Times*, June 1974.

5. Twila Van Leer, "State Honors Team That Saved Tot from Near-Certain Death," *Deseret News*, September 23, 1986.

6. Thomas Carlile, MD, "Self-Administered Heimlich Maneuver," *Journal of the American Medical Association* 249, no. 23 (June 17, 1983): 3175.

7. "Simple Method Relieves Café Coronary," *Journal of the American Medical Association* 229, no. 4 (August 12, 1974): 746–47.

8. Henry J. Heimlich, MD, "A Life-Saving Maneuver to Prevent Food-Choking," *Journal of the American Medical Association* 234, no. 4 (October 27, 1975): 398–401.

9. "Statement on the 'Heimlich Maneuver,'" *Journal of the American Medical Association* 234, no. 4 (October 27, 1975): 416.

10. Woody Allen, "A Giant Step for Mankind," *New Yorker*, June 9, 1980, pp. 36–38.

11. "Voices: Seventies Speak," *Life*, December 1979, p. 16.

12. Sarah Hardee, "Heimlich Honors an Older Brother for Saving Little One," *Cincinnati Enquirer*, March 14, 2013, sec. C.

CHAPTER 14. THE AMERICAN RED CROSS AND BACK BLOWS

1. Jean Carper, "Beware the Back Slap If You're Choking to Death," *Washington Post*, April 22, 1979, p. C1; Henry J. Heimlich, MD, "First Aid for Choking: Back Blows and Chest Thrusts Cause Complications and Death," *Neo Reviews* 70, no. 1 (July 1, 1982): 120–25.

2. S. Boussuges, "Use of the Heimlich Maneuver on Children in the Rhône-Alpes Area," abstract, *Archives francaises de Pediatrie* 42, no. 8 (1985): 733–36.

3. "Our Federal Charter," American Red Cross, http://www.redcross.org/about-us/history/federal-charter (accessed July 19, 2013).

4. Ibid.

5. "Take a Class," American Red Cross, http://www.redcross.org/take-a-class (accessed July 17, 2013).

6. Ed Grabianowski, "How the American Red Cross Works," *HowStuffWorks. com*, http://money.howstuffworks.com/american-red-cross3.htm (accessed July 17, 2013).

7. G. F. Tucker Jr., "Report of the Committee for the Prevention of Foreign Body Accidents," *Trans Am Bronchoesophagol Assoc* 49 (1969): 181.

8. David Montoya, MD, MCFP, FRCPC, "Management of the Choking Victim," *Canadian Medical Association Journal* 135, no. 4 (August 15, 1986): 305–11.

9. Henry J. Heimlich, MD, "A Life-Saving Maneuver to Prevent Food-Choking," *Journal of the American Medical Association* 234, no. 4 (October 27, 1975): 398–401.

10. Charles Wayne Guildner, Doug Williams, and Tom Subitch, "Airway Obstructed by Foreign Material: The Heimlich Maneuver," *Journal of the American College of Emergency Physicians* 5, no. 9 (1976): 676.

11. International Medical News Service, "Heimlich Calls Modification of 'Maneuver' Dangerous," *Pediatric News* (October 1976): 20.

12. Archer S. Gordon et al., "Emergency Management of Foreign Body Airway Obstruction," in *Advances in Cardiopulmonary Resuscitation*, ed. Peter Safar (New York: Springer-Verlag, 1977), pp. 39–40.

13. Ibid.

14. Guildner, Williams, and Subitch, "Airway Obstructed by Foreign Material."

15. B. R. Fink, "Biomechanics of Upper Airway Obstruction" (lecture, National Research Council Emergency Airway Management Conference, Washington, DC, 1976).

16. Carper, "Beware the Back Slap If You're Choking to Death."

17. Richard L. Day, Edmund S. Crelin, and Arthur B. DuBois, "Choking: The Heimlich Abdominal Thrust vs. Back Blows: An Approach to Measurement of Inertial and Aerodynamic Forces," *Pediatrics* 70, no. 1 (1982): 117–18.

18. Cristine Russell, "Heimlich Maneuver Endorsed," *Washington Post*, October 2, 1985, p. A9.

19. Ibid.

20. C. Everett Koop, MD, ScD, "The Heimlich Maneuver," *Public Health Reports* 100, no. 6 (November/December 1985): 557.

21. "The American Red Cross Unveils Innovative New First Aid and CPR/AED Training Programs," American Red Cross, news release, April 4, 2006, http://web .archive.org/web/20060429202036/http://www.redcross.org/pressrelease/0,1077 ,0_314 _5262,00.html (accessed July 17, 2013).

22. Robert A. Berg, "2010 American Heart Association and American Red Cross Guidelines for First Aid," *Circulation* 122 (2010): S696.

23. "Conscious Choking," American Red Cross, http://www.redcross.org/flash/ brr/English-html/conscious-choking.asp (accessed July 17, 2013).

24. Joan Nathan, "A Heimlich in Every Pot," *New York Times*, February 4, 2009, p. A31.

25. A. Soroudi et al., "Adult Foreign Body Airway Obstruction in the Prehospital Setting," abstract, *Prehospital Emergency Care* 11, no. 1 (2007): 25–29.

26. Liam Thorp, "Woman Dies after Choking on Food at Royal Balti House in Farnworth," *Bolton News*, July 24, 2013, http://www.theboltonnews.co.uk/ news/10567426.Woman_dies_after_choking_on_food_at_Indian_restaurant/ (accessed July 30, 2013).

27. Carper, "Beware the Back Slap If You're Choking to Death."

CHAPTER 15. THE GIFT OF BREATH: THE HEIMLICH MICROTRACH

1. "FAQs," National Lung Health Education Program, http://www.nlhep.org/Pages/FAQS.aspx (accessed July 19, 2013).

2. Thomas L. Petty, MD; Robert W. McCoy, BS, RRT; and Dennis E. Doherty, MD, "Long Term Oxygen Therapy (LTOT)," National Lung Health Education Program, http://www.nlhep.org/Documents/lt_oxygen.pdf (accessed July 19, 2013).

3. Henry Heimlich, MD, "Respiratory Rehabilitation with Transtracheal Oxygen System," *Annals of Otology, Rhinology and Laryngology* 91, no. 6 (November/December 1982): 644.

4. H. J. Heimlich, "Oxygen Delivery for Ambulatory Patients. How the Micro-Trach Increases Mobility," *Postgraduate Medicine* 84, no. 6 (November 1, 1988): 68–73.

5. Thomas Stuber, interview by Dr. Henry J. Heimlich, *The Real Me*, Good Life TV, November 16, 1999.

6. Ibid.

7. John Kosowatz, "'I Call It the Heimlich Miracle,'" *Bridgeport Telegram*, April 30, 1982, p. 4.

8. Ibid.

9. Gwen Kelly, "Illness, Surgery Fail to Delay Determined Couple's Wedding," *Shreveport Times* (March 3, 1990).

10. Ibid.

11. Ned Martel, "Heimlich's Next Maneuver," *Naples Daily News*, May 28, 1991, pp. D1, D4.

12. Ibid.

13. B. S. Bloom et al., "Transtracheal Oxygen Delivery and Patients with Chronic Obstructive Pulmonary Disease," *Respiratory Medicine* 83, no. 4 (1989): 281–88.

14. Milan Korcok, "Delivering Oxygen Transtracheally May Be a Boon for COPD Patients," *Journal of the American Medical Association* 248, no. 2 (July 9, 1982): 153–54.

15. Ibid.

16. H. J. Heimlich and G. C. Carr, "The Micro-Trach. A Seven-Year Experience with Transtracheal Oxygen Therapy," *Chest* 95, no. 5 (May 1989): 1008–1012.

CHAPTER 16. MAKING THE MOST OF GOOD IDEAS

*When we performed the malariotherapy research in China, all patients involved in the study, as in all of our research studies at the Heimlich Institute, granted their permission to participate. We chose China as a location partly because there was a readily available source of malaria there, which was not found in the United States. Official approval for carrying out the study was granted by the Municipal Department of Health of Guangzhou, by the Provincial Department of Health of Guangdong Province, and by the Provincial Committee of Science and Technology of Guangdong Province. On June 8, 2000, Steven A. Masiello, director of the Office of Compliance and Biologics Quality in the Center for Biologics Evaluation and Research in the Department of Health and Human Services' Food and Drug Administration, sent me a letter by certified mail stating that "regulatory authorities in the People's Republic of China . . . is the appropriate authority for oversight of such foreign research, not a United States based IRB [Institutional Review Board]."

1. Lou Carlozo, "Heimlich Maneuvers into Safety Hall of Fame," *Chicago Tribune*, October 5, 1993, http://articles.chicagotribune.com/1993-10-05/news/9310050180 _1_heimlich-maneuver-henry-j-heimlich-mrs-dole (accessed November 13, 2013).

2. Arthur Snider, "New Hug Can Save Drowning Victim," *Chicago Daily News*, August 24, 1974, pp. 1, 6.

3. Ibid.

4. "2010, United States Unintentional Drowning Deaths and Rates per 100,000: All Races, Both Sexes, All Ages," Centers for Disease Control and Prevention, National Center for Injury Prevention and Control.

5. "Protect the Ones You Love: Child Injuries Are Preventable," Centers for Disease Control and Prevention, National Center for Injury Prevention and Control, Division of Unintentional Injury Prevention, last updated April 19, 2012, http://www.cdc.gov/safechild/NAP/background.html (accessed July 17, 2013).

6. "Injury Prevention & Control: Data & Statistics (WISQARS)," Centers for Disease Control and Prevention, National Center for Injury Prevention and Control, http://www.cdc.gov/injury/wisqars/index.html (accessed July 17, 2013).

7. "2010 American Heart Association and American Red Cross Guidelines for First Aid," *Circulation* 122 (2010): S934–S936.

8. N. Manolios and I. Mackie, "Drowning and Near-Drowning on Australian Beaches Patrolled by Life-Savers: A 10-Year Study, 1973–1983," *Medical Journal of Australia* 148, no. 4 (1988): 165.

9. E. F. Van Beeck et al., "Policy and Practice," *Bulletin of the World Health Organization* 83, no. 11 (November 2011): 855.

10. Joseph P. Ornato, "The Resuscitation of Near-Drowning Victims," *Journal of the American Medical Association* 256, no. 1 (1986): 75.

11. Jerome H. Modell, "Drowning," *New England Journal of Medicine* 328, no. 4 (1993): 253–56.

12. Snider, "New Hug Can Save Drowning Victim."

13. Karen MacGrogan, "Pair Honored for Heimlich Rescue," *Destin Log*, December 9, 1989, pp. 1A, 3A.

14. "An Open Letter to Our Client, the Public and the Press," National Aquatic Safety Company, http://nascoaquatics.com/?page_id=1273 (accessed August 13, 2013).

15. Ibid.

16. Staff of the National Aquatics Safety Company, LLC, "Unconscious or Passive Victims," *NASCO Lifeguard Textbook*, http://nascoaquatics.com/wp-content/uploads/2012/02/lifeguard-textbook-2012.pdf (accessed August 16, 2013), p. 76.

17. John L. Hunsucker, "NASCO Press Release," August 12, 2009, http://www.scribd.com/doc/49537320/8-12-09-NASCO-press-release-re-misleading-and-prejudicial-media-statements (accessed November 13, 2013), p. 1.

18. Manolios and Mackie, "Drowning and Near-Drowning on Australian Beaches Patrolled by Life-Savers," pp. 165–71.

19. James P. Orlowski, "Vomiting as a Complication of the Heimlich Maneuver," *Journal of the American Medical Association* 258, no. 4 (1987): 512–13.

20. Ibid, pp. 2–3.

21. John Fauber, "Advair: How Safe Is This Drug?" MedPageToday.com, November 18, 2012, http://www.medpagetoday.com/AllergyImmunology/Asthma/36000 (accessed July 17, 2013).

22. "Heimlich Maneuver Saves Asthma Sufferers," *Caring World*, 1999, p. 2.

23. Stephen M. Feanny, Anne St. John, and P. Howard, "Utilisation of the Heimlich Maneuver as an Adjunct in the Management of Asthma in Paediatric Patients: A Prospective Study," abstract, *West Indian Medical Journal* 54 (2005): 45.

24. For a clip from the episode, see "Everest - The Death Zone (Part One)," YouTube video, 14:46, from PBS's *Nova*, posted by "TheWorldIsBiggerThanMe," September 8, 2011, http://www.youtube.com/watch?v=YC9sBo1WHXA (accessed July 17, 2013).

25. Henry Heimlich, MD, "Respiratory Rehabilitation with Transtracheal Oxygen System," *Annals of Otology, Rhinology and Laryngology* 91, no. 6 (November/December 1982): 643–47.

26. Ibid.

27. "Julius Wagner-Jauregg," *Nobel Lectures, Physiology or Medicine 1922–1941* (Amsterdam, Neth.: Elsevier Publishing, 1965).

28. E. Chernin, "The Malariatherapy of Neurosyphilis," *Journal of Parasitology* 70 (1984): 611–17.

29. "HIV/AIDS Basic Statistics," Centers for Disease Control and Prevention, Division of HIV/AIDS Prevention, National Center for HIV/AIDS, Viral Hepatitis, Sexual Transmitted Diseases and Tuberculosis Prevention, http://www.cdc.gov/hiv/basics/statistics.html (accessed July 18, 2013).

30. Ibid.

31. Ibid.

32. "HIV/AIDS Facts," GreaterThanOne.org, San Francisco AIDS foundation, last updated February 2011, http://greaterthanone.org/about/hivaids-facts.html (accessed July 18, 2013).

33. "Global Effort to Halt and Reverse HIV/AIDS Showing Results, Finds UN Report," UN News Centre, November 23, 2010, http://www.un.org/apps/news/story.asp/html/story.asp?NewsID=36842&Cr=hiv&Cr1=#.UnH3QRYjPFE (accessed October 31, 2013).

34. "How We're Spending," AIDS.gov, US Department of Health and Human Services, last revised July 5, 2013, http://aids.gov/federal-resources/funding-opportunities/how-were-spending/ (accessed July 18, 2013).

35. David Wessner, "What Does HIV/AIDS Cost? The Answer to This Question Depends a Lot on Whom You Ask," *The AIDS Pandemic* (blog), October 26, 2010, http://the-aids-pandemic.blogspot.com/2010/10/what-does-hivaids-cost-answer-to-this.html (accessed July 17, 2013).

36. Henry J. Heimlich et al., "Malariotherapy for HIV Patients," *Mechanisms of Ageing and Development* 93, no. 1 (1997): 79–85.

37. Xiaoping Chen et al., "Phase-1 Studies of Malariotherapy for HIV Infection," *Chinese Medical Sciences Journal/Chinese Academy of Medical Sciences* 14, no. 4 (1999): 224–28.

38. Alan E. Greenberg et al., "Plasmodium Falciparum Malaria and Perinatally Acquired Human Immunodeficiency Virus Type 1 Infection in Kinshasa, Zaire: A Prospective, Longitudinal Cohort Study of 587 Children," *New England Journal of Medicine* 325, no. 2 (1991): 105–109.

CHAPTER 17. WORKING TOWARD A CARING WORLD

1. David Brown, "Todd Frazier Performs Heimlich Maneuver, Saves Choking Man at Lunch," Yahoo! Sports, May 29, 2012, http://sports.yahoo.com/blogs/mlb-big-league-stew/todd-frazier-performs-heimlich-maneuver-saves-chokingman-013455303.html (accessed November 2, 2013).

2. Kate Nolan, "Innovations in Medicine: Originator of Heimlich Maneuver to Be Here Today," *Chautauqua Daily*, July 6, 1983.

3. Henry J. Heimlich et al., "Apollo Double Diaphragm Pump for Use in Artificial Heart-Lung Systems" (AAMI National Meeting, March 20, 1975).

4. "'A Caring World,' the Slogan of Heimlich." *Iran News*, May 11, 1998, p. 11.

5. Rick Gladstone, "U.S. Envoy Optimistic About Ties with China," *New York Times*, December 18, 2012, p. A12.

6. Cliff Peale, "UC Plans New Campus—7,600 Miles away in China," *Enquirer*, June 7, 2013.

7. Xuemao Wang, dean and university librarian, University of Cincinnati, conversation with Dr. Heimlich, November 20, 2013.

INDEX